D0514865

PAPERTOY MONSTERS

50 Cool Papertoys You Can Make Yourself!

CASTLEFORTE

and 24 of the Top Papertoy Designers from Around the World

PAPERTOY

CASTLEFORTE

and 24 of the Top Papertoy Designers
from Around the World

MONSTERS

WORKMAN PUBLISHING ■ **NEW YORK**

I would like to dedicate this book to my beautiful wife, Linda, and my amazing fur child—
my dog—Soul. They are the two biggest loves and inspirations in my life.

Also to my very good friend, Super Cooper, my biggest fan, the #1 papertoy lover on the
planet, and the coolest kid I have ever known. He inspires my inner child, keeping my old man
locked up tight and out of sight. This book is for you, buddy.

And to his beautiful little sister Bella, who brings pure joy to my heart every day.

Library of Congress Cataloging-in-Publication Data is available.

ISBN 978-0-7611-5882-0

Written by Brian Castleforte
Design by Netta Rabin
Illustrations by Robert James
Photography by Jen Browning and Netta Rabin

Workman books are available at special discounts when purchased in bulk for premiums and sales promotions as well as for
fund-raising or educational use. Special editions or book excerpts also can be created to specification. For details,
contact the Special Sales Director at the address below or send an e-mail to specialsales@workman.com.

Workman Publishing Company, Inc.
225 Varick Street
New York, NY 10014-4381
www.workman.com

Printed in China
First printing October 2010

10 9 8 7 6 5 4

ACKNOWLEDGMENTS

A big thanks to each and every artist involved in making this book.
For your incredible talents and hard work,
and for being such a powerful force in the papertoy community.

Thank you to Netta Rabin for bringing this project to me,
and for helping me to make it amazing.

Thank you to my editor, Raquel Jaramillo,
for helping an artist to become a bit of a writer.

Thanks to everyone else at Workman Publishing
for helping to make this incredible book a reality.

Thanks to Johnny and Greg, Cooper and Bella, for being the most amazing,
inspirational, and loving fans, friends, and family I could ever hope to have.

Thanks to all of my friends who have visited my sites and downloaded
my papertoys over the years. You are the reason I keep doing what I do.

Thanks to all of the members at NicePaperToys.com
for helping to make the papertoy community more
incredible than ever, and for keeping it so NICE!

Thanks to Sjors Trimbach, for creating the first papertoy
I ever built, Brickboy, which inspired my first papertoys.

Thanks to YOU! All of you who bought this book—
papertoy creators, fans, and collectors.
You are why we made it. I hope you love it.

And finally, a huge thank you to all of my friends and family,
who have never stopped believing in me, inspiring me, and putting up with me,
in all of my creative endeavors. Especially you, Linda.

Contents

Gene Chemzyme, p. 61

Pharaoh Thoth Amon, p. 47

MONSTER LEGENDS

EARTH, OCEAN & SPACE MONSTERS

Wingy Wingy, p. 113

Paulette, p. 201

The Experiment, p. 193

Introduction

WHEN I WAS A KID, THERE WERE TWO THINGS that always seemed to excite me more than anything else. One was toys, of course. Not surprising: What kid doesn't like toys? But the toys I liked the most were the creative ones, the kind that let me bring my ideas to life. Legos. Etch A Sketch. Play-Doh. Toys I could make or put together.

THE SECOND THING I LIKED MOST IN THE WORLD was monsters. Godzilla. King Kong. Bigfoot. Frankenstein. I enjoyed the cute and silly variety, too, the kind you might find on a cereal box. Frankenberry. Count Chocula. I was partial to the monsters on *Scooby-Doo* as well.

AT SOME POINT, I BEGAN COMBINING MY TWO passions and started sketching and building my own toy monsters using my favorite Legos and Play-Doh. I liked playing the mad scientist and seeing how crazy my ideas could get.

MY INTEREST DIDN'T WANE AT ALL AS I GREW older. In fact, monsters became something of an obsession for me, and I wondered how I could bring my sketches to life as toys. I became involved in the vinyl art movement, but I soon discovered that,

cool as it is to have your very own toys produced, it's a very expensive thing to do.

SO I STARTED SEEKING OUT ALTERNATIVES. AND then—*bam!*—I found the answer. I stumbled onto a website by Norwegian artist Sjors. He had created this amazing little creature called Brickboy out of nothing more than small paper cubes. It was unbelievable. What's more, Sjors provided a free, downloadable blank template that people could customize to create their own monsters! Well, you better believe I downloaded that template just as fast as my modem would allow, and with a few modifications, my first papertoy was born.

I CALLED HIM NICEBUNNY. AND THAT WAS THE start of something that would change my life forever: papertoys. I ended up making a set of five Nicebunny papertoys, and they were a big hit. All of a sudden my obscure little antihero bunny was all over the world, living on the desks of more people than I could imagine. It was, quite literally, my dream come true.

AMAZED BY THE POSSIBILITY OF SUCH VAST and relatively easy—not to mention extremely cheap—distribution, I proceeded to develop an original series of papertoys that I called Hedcase. It was a simple, easy-to-build model for which an original "skin," or design for an existing template, could be added every week via a new download. Hedcase quickly became popular, so I released a blank template, allowing anyone to make his or her own Hedcase toy with a customized skin.

AT THIS POINT, I REALIZED THAT THESE LITTLE papertoys were becoming much bigger than anything I could have anticipated: a new art form, a way to create a toy out of hardly more than a sheet of paper and a lot of imagination.

I STARTED THE WEBSITE NICEPAPERTOYS.COM, where fans and artists all over the world could bounce ideas off each other and showcase their creations. The papertoy movement really is the ultimate community-based art form: People share in a way that is truly inspiring. What started out as a smattering of artists making strange, never-before-seen papertoys for one another has exploded into a community of thousands of enthusiasts, fanatics, collectors, and creators. It's a testament to the ever expanding papertoy universe.

THE PAPERTOYS IN THIS BOOK were created by 24 of my favorite artists from around the world, and I contributed two of my own designs. Each monster has his or her own unique personality, of course, and a name, a biography, a history—you'll see that half the fun of creating a papertoy is inventing a character for it.

SINCE SOME OF YOU ARE BRAND-NEW TO THE world of papertoys, I've made sure to include some monsters that are easy to make, as well as some that are not so easy. Start with the simplest ones and, once you feel confident, move on to the more difficult toys. The cool thing about this book—besides all the papertoys!—is that the templates are printed on special paper that's easy to fold and glue. They are perforated, so all you need to do is pop one out and start folding. And because they are scored, you'll get good, clean folds, which is very important in the construction of lasting papertoys.

ENOUGH TALK ABOUT WHY I LOVE PAPERTOYS— it's time to learn how to make them!

How to Build Your Papertoys

Constructing a papertoy monster is simple and easy once you get the hang of it. Here are some general instructions and helpful hints to get you started.

WHAT YOU'LL DEFINITELY NEED

GLUE: glue sticks are the easiest and least messy option, but white glue or any craft glue that works with paper may be used.

OPTIONAL TOOLS

PEN OR PENCIL: helpful when you need to curve a template. Also useful to hold down tabs inside a toy while you wait for them to dry.

TWEEZERS: for handling small templates and tabs.

SMOOTH, JUMBO PAPER CLIP: helpful to reach remaining tabs that may need to be glued on the inside of a closed template.

SPOON: you can use the rounded part to curve a template, and the handle to hold any small tabs in place until the glue dries or to help you make crisp folds.

INSTRUCTIONS

DETACH the first template(s) according to the specific instructions for each papertoy.

FOLD the template on all the precreased fold lines, pressing down firmly to make nice, crisp folds.

There are two types of folds:

NORMAL FOLDS—or mountain folds—look like a mountain or a capital A. Almost all of your folds will be normal, unless they are marked otherwise.

VALLEY FOLDS look like a valley or the letter V. Very few of your folds will be a valley, but make sure to keep an eye out for them! Look for fold lines marked like this: —.—.—.—.—

GLUE all numbered tabs to the corresponding numbered gray areas (or glue numbered gray areas to each other) in numerical order (1, 2, 3, and so on), as directed in the instructions. Be patient—make sure to hold glued areas together long enough for the glue to dry so that your model remains intact and strong.

REPEAT these steps for each piece of the toy until you have completed your papertoy monster.

Your Very Own Papertoys

ALL YOU NEED TO BEGIN YOUR JOURNEY INTO the world of papertoys is this book, some glue, a little time, and an understanding of the basic rules. That's it!

Once you have mastered the art of building other people's papertoys, you might feel ready to make your own. Start by using the blank templates at the back of the book, customizing—or "skinning"— them to create your own papertoy monster variations. This is a great way to learn the basics of papertoy design.

When you've become comfortable "skinning" existing templates, you are ready to begin making your own templates. I suggest starting with the basics: simple cubes and cones. See what you can come up with, making additions or alterations as needed. There is no right or wrong way to design papertoys. Every artist has a different method. Some use 3-D software, but many just keep drawing, cutting, folding, and gluing until they get it right. Some really complex toys are made of many parts and require two or three templates, while others are designed as a single piece. It is really up to you how you choose to design your toy.

Papertoys are like monsters—all are different, many are imperfect, but each and every one is special in its own way. Hmmm, sounds a bit like people. Maybe that's why papertoy monsters seem so special.

Once you have a papertoy of your own that you're really proud of, and you're ready to share it with the world, log on to my website, nicepapertoys.com, and create your own profile page. It's easy, and it's free! Then you can upload your pictures, share your templates, meet other artists and fans, and lots more.

So that's about it, everyone. Let's not keep these monsters waiting any longer. Go ahead and choose the one you want to start with and get busy. You have 50 monsters to set free from the pages of this book.

Have fun and happy folding!

Castleforte

Castleforte's first sketch of Confetti Yeti

His second sketch with color

The final sketch with a scarier face!

ICY HUGGY

TYPE: *Monstrum legendarus nix yeticus*

VARIANT NAMES: Yeti; Abominable Snowman

ORIGIN: Himalayas

DESCRIPTION: 10 feet tall; dangling beard; 1,023 pounds

ABILITIES: runs fast; leaps over canyons in a single bound; can drink an entire lake in one gulp

ICY HUGGY

Discovered by Salazad

ASSEMBLY INSTRUCTIONS

A Detach HEAD and BEARD templates. Insert tab 1 on BEARD into slot under mouth on HEAD and glue to gray area 1.

B Detach TAIL template. Insert tabs 2–3 into slots on back of HEAD and glue to gray areas 2–3.

C Glue tabs 4–14 on HEAD to gray areas 4–14.

D Detach RIGHT ARM template. Glue tabs 15–24 to gray areas 15–24.

E Detach LEFT ARM template. Glue tabs 25–34 to gray areas 25–34.

F Glue RIGHT ARM to HEAD at gray area 35.

G Glue LEFT ARM to HEAD at gray area 36.

First things first! Remember to fold on all creases before you glue.

Icy Huggy is a long-bearded snow monster from somewhere in the Himalayas, where he lives in a cave on a mountain of ice. Friendly (though a tad on the shy side), Icy is a very fast runner and is able to use his powerful legs to leap from mountaintop to mountaintop. His favorite hobby is sled-singing: sledding down a mountain on your back while singing very loudly. When Icy sled-sings, mountain climbers often mistake the sound for a piercing growl, leading to endless stories about an "abominable snowman" living atop the mountain. Icy is neither abominable nor a snowman, but he does love making snow angels. If you see Icy Huggy, do not be afraid. Offer him an apple and he will be your friend for life.

SCARLEAH

TYPE: *Monstrum legendarus goblinitas*

VARIANT NAMES: The Witch Monster; Goblina

ORIGIN: Edina, Minnesota, U.S.A.

DESCRIPTION: green skin; red eyes; purple suit and hat

ABILITIES: crafting dastardly spells; flying through the air on her specially equipped broom

SCARLEAH

Discovered by Jason Harlan

ASSEMBLY INSTRUCTIONS

A Detach BODY template. Glue tabs 1–8 to gray areas 1–8.

B Detach RIGHT ARM and LEFT ARM templates. Glue gray areas 9 and 10 on RIGHT and LEFT ARMS to gray areas 9 and 10 on BODY.

C Detach HAT TOP template. Glue tab 11 to gray area 11.

D Detach HAT BASE template. Glue tabs 12–13 on HAT TOP to gray areas 12–13 on HAT BASE.

E Glue HAT BASE to BODY at gray area 14.

Scarleah is an unpleasant goblin witch with green skin, glowing red eyes, and sharp, fanged teeth that she often uses when hunting for rodents and small beasts. On humans she prefers to use the evil incantations she learned from an ancient book of dark spells that she inherited as a young witchling. These spells, gathered throughout the centuries by the goblin witches who came before her, make humans hopelessly stupid. Scarleah lives beyond the Kobold Kingdom, past the seven Rivers of Solitude in a place known as the Cavern of Infinite Woe, which is found at the top of the highest mountain, in the Hollow Hills section of Edina, Minnesota. No one who has sought her has ever returned. CLASSIFIED

HOORGUEN

Bon appétit

TYPE: Monstrum legendarus ogrensis
VARIANT NAMES: The Giant; The Ogre from Skye
ORIGIN: Isle of Skye, Scotland
DESCRIPTION: 40 feet tall; green beard; yellow teeth
ABILITIES: quick as lightning; devours children in 1.2 seconds flat

Bon appétit

Discovered by Jérôme Thieulin, aka Jerom

ASSEMBLY INSTRUCTIONS

A Detach HEAD template. Glue tabs 1–7 to gray areas 1–7.

B Detach UPPER JAW template. Glue tabs 8–14 to gray areas 8–14.

C Detach BODY template. Glue tabs 15–19 to gray areas 15–19.

D Detach BACK template. Glue HEAD to BACK at gray area 20. Glue UPPER JAW to BACK at gray area 21. Glue BODY to BACK at gray area 22.

Hoorgue, an ogre monster, has six very large—and fast—legs, two mouths, and three stomachs. Roughly as tall as a three-story house, Hoorgue has no trouble catching his favorite prey: giant children. These ten-foot-tall kids can be found roaming wild and in great abundance in Giant Country on the Isle of Skye, in the Scottish Highlands, and though they live in mortal fear of Hoorgue, they still love to tease and torment him whenever possible. They call him names like "Smelly Hoorgue" or "Hoorgue the Six-Legged Poop," and they throw small boulders at him when he's hungrily chasing after them.

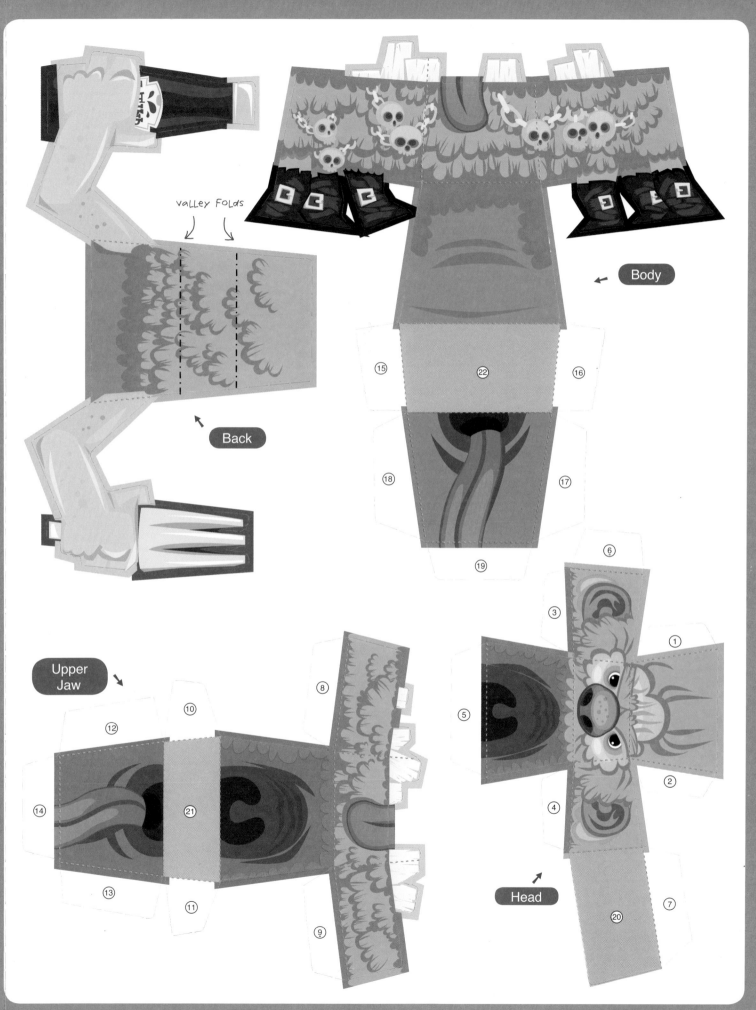

valley folds

Body

Back

Upper Jaw

Head

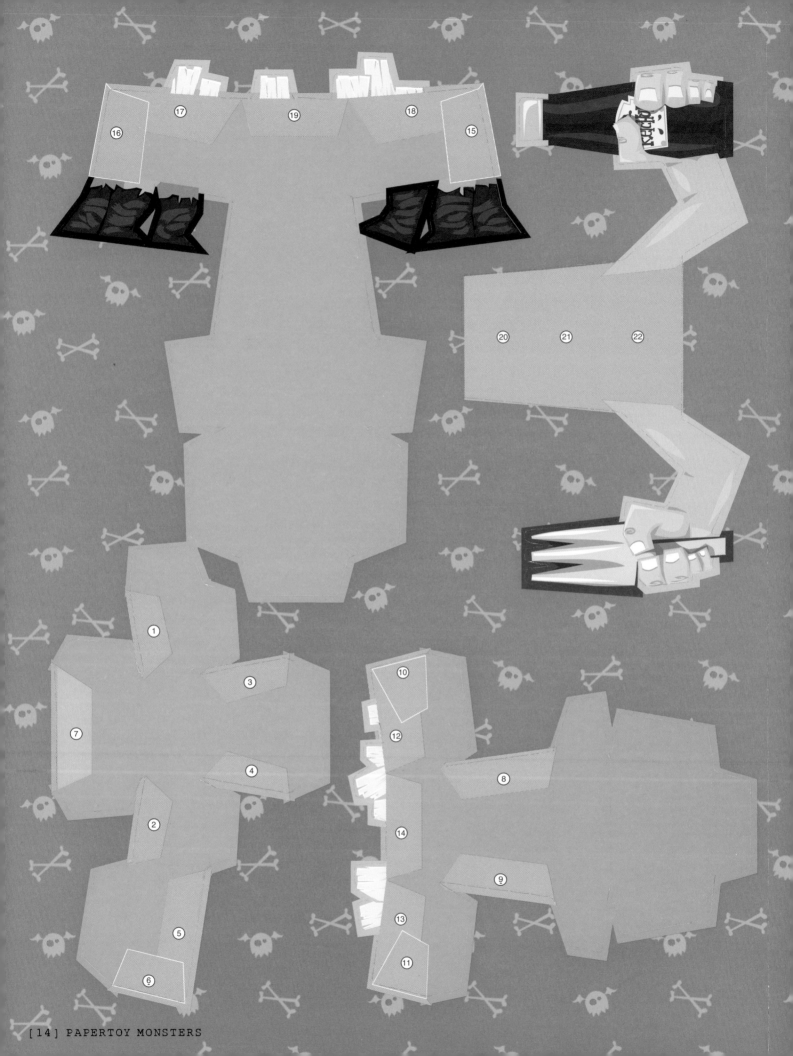

the Gloog Pack

TYPE: *Monstrum legendarius phantasmicus*

VARIANT NAMES: The Ghosts Monster, Les Boooo

ORIGIN: Ostend, Belgium

DESCRIPTION: a blob of mustached ghosts

ABILITIES: flying; absorbing the souls of humans; creating the perfect handlebar mustache

Discovered by Jérôme Thieulin, aka Jerom

ASSEMBLY INSTRUCTIONS

A Detach HEAD template. Glue tabs 1–6 to gray areas 1–6.

B Detach BODY template. Glue tab 7 to gray area 7.

C Glue tabs 8–9 on HEAD to gray areas 8–9 on BODY.

D Glue tabs 10–11 on BODY to gray areas 10–11 on HEAD.

E Insert tab 12 on BODY into slot on bottom of BODY and glue to gray area 12.

F Detach TAIL template. Glue tab 13 to gray area 13.

G Detach GRAVE template. Insert tab 14 on TAIL into slot on side of GRAVE and glue to gray area 14.

H Glue tab 15 on GRAVE to gray area 15.

I Glue tab 16 on TAIL to gray area 16 on BODY.

J Detach FRONT SECTION and GHOST A–D templates. Curve GHOSTS and insert tabs 17–20 into slots on sides of FRONT SECTION and glue to gray areas 17–20.

K Glue tabs 21–23 on BODY to gray areas 21–23 on FRONT SECTION.

L Glue tabs 24–25 on TAIL to gray areas 24–25 on FRONT SECTION.

Almost two centuries ago, three dozen Belgian miners tragically lost their lives when the poorly secured mine they were excavating caved in on them. The mine was owned by a greedy industrial baron named Piquot, known throughout Europe as Baron Mustache because under his nose he wore an enormous mustache, which he was fond of twirling in a dastardly manner. For 180 years, the tormented souls of these miners have haunted the grounds above the mine searching for the soul of Baron Mustache in the hope of exacting their vengeance. The locals call this terrifying mass of angry ghosts the Gloomy Pack. Not only does this blob of phantasms fly around screaming and shrieking at the top of its various gelatinous lungs, it also absorbs the souls of any humans foolish enough to get near it. Luckily for the locals, the Gloomy Pack is easily distinguished from other hordes of flying ghosts because of its mustaches, which bear a striking resemblance to the baron's.

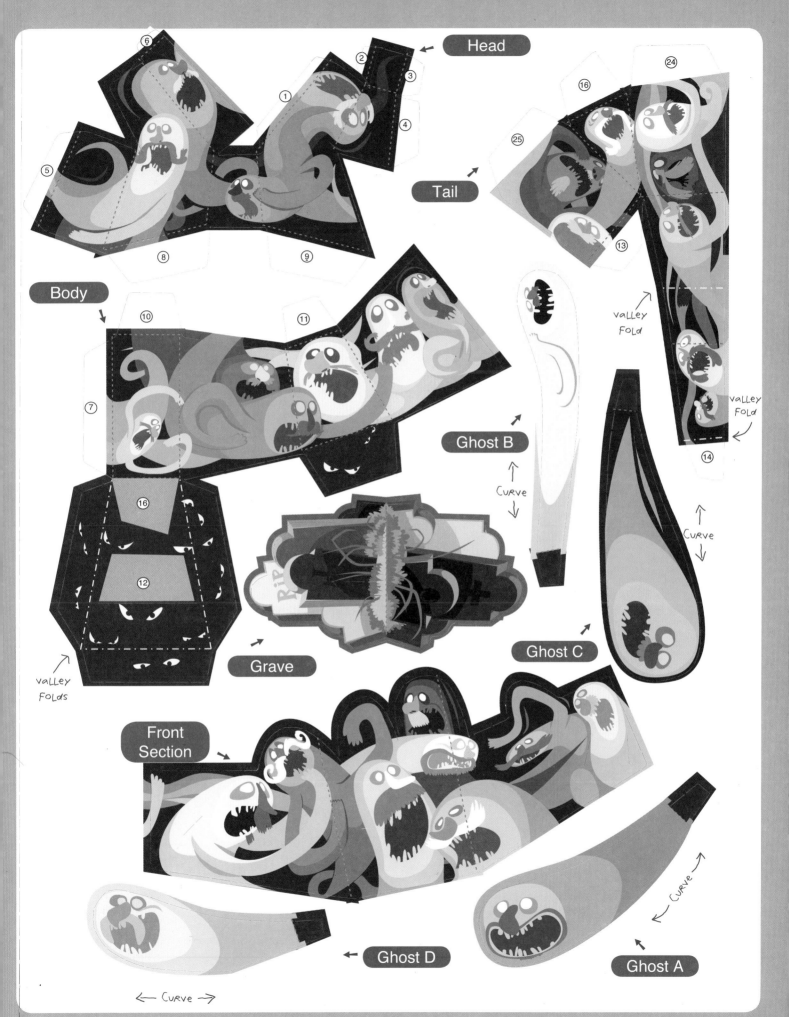

Head

Tail

Body

valley
fold

valley
fold

Ghost B

Curve

Curve

valley
folds

Grave

Ghost C

Front
Section

Ghost D

Ghost A

← Curve →

Curve →

← Curve

Medusa

TYPE: *Monstrum legendarus gorgonus*

VARIANT NAME: Snake Girl (said behind her back)

ORIGIN: Miami, Florida, U.S.A.

DESCRIPTION: 5 feet tall, petite, green hair with snakes

ABILITIES: turning humans to stone, backflips, finding the best sales in a 550-mile radius

Medusa

Discovered by Jonny Chiba

ASSEMBLY INSTRUCTIONS

A Detach BODY template. Glue tabs 1–11 to gray areas 1–11.

B Detach TAIL template. Glue tab 12 to gray area 12 on BODY.

C Detach ARMS template. Insert tab 13 into slot on top of BODY.

D Detach HEAD template. Curve top of HEAD and glue tabs 14–20 to gray areas 14–20.

E Insert tab 21 on ARMS into slot on bottom of HEAD.

Medusa, a gorgon monster, is a direct descendant of the original Medusa of ancient Greek mythology. Shallow and self-obsessed, Medusa is able to pass for an ordinary teenage girl, and she is the head cheerleader of the Titans, a high school football team in Miami. Medusa lives in a mall, where she spends most of her time shopping for shoes and clothes during the day. At night she can be found straightening her coily snake-hair so that it will flip nicely during cheerleading practice the next day. Bubbly, silly, and fiercely hostile to any girls she thinks are prettier than she is (which is almost all of them), Medusa inherited her ancestor's ability to turn humans into stone with a single icy look. She can also do three backflips in a row.

Wolfman Joe

TYPE: *Monstrum legendarus lupus*

VARIANT NAMES: The Werewolf; The Furry Enforcer

ORIGIN: Chicago, Illinois, U.S.A.

DESCRIPTION: 7 feet tall; covered in fur

ABILITIES: can follow someone's scent up to 40 miles away; has a perfect backstroke

Wolfman Joe

Discovered by Nana Pong, aka Roomism

ASSEMBLY INSTRUCTIONS

A Detach LEFT BODY and FRONT BODY templates. Glue tabs 1–7 on LEFT BODY to gray areas 1–7 on FRONT BODY.

B Detach RIGHT BODY template. Glue tabs 8–14 to gray areas 8–14 on FRONT BODY.

C Detach INSEAM template. Glue tabs 15–25 to gray areas 15–25 on FRONT BODY.

D Glue tab 26 on INSEAM to gray area 26 on LEFT BODY.

E Glue tab 27 on INSEAM to gray area 27 on RIGHT BODY.

F Detach BACK BODY template. Glue tabs 28–49 on body piece to gray areas 28–49 on BACK BODY.

G Detach HEAD and LEFT SNOUT templates. Glue tabs 50–58 on HEAD to gray areas 50–58 on LEFT SNOUT.

H Detach RIGHT SNOUT template. Glue tabs 59–67 on HEAD to gray areas 59–67 on RIGHT SNOUT.

I Glue tab 68 on RIGHT SNOUT to gray area 68 on HEAD. Glue tab 69 on HEAD to gray area 69 on HEAD. Glue tab 70 on LEFT SNOUT to gray area 70 on HEAD.

J Glue HEAD to FRONT BODY at gray area 71.

K Detach RIGHT ARM template. Glue tab 72 to gray area 72 on RIGHT BODY.

L Detach LEFT ARM template. Glue tab 73 to gray area 73 on LEFT BODY.

Born in Chicago in 1905, Wolfman Joe started working as a brute enforcer for Chicago's North Side mob in his early 20s. It was during an attempt to "rub out" Al Capone that Wolfman Joe encountered the "dogs" that would forever alter his life. The moon was full that night. Joe tracked Capone to an abandoned warehouse, where he hoped to surprise the Capone mob. Instead, a pack of huge, vicious dogs attacked him, biting him repeatedly before he was able to escape. A few days later, the transformation began: His skin started growing fur, his voice became deeper, and his teeth grew long. Within a year he went from a human being to a true wolf. Unlike other werewolves, which change only during full moons, Wolfman Joe is always a wolf. He has retained the ability to speak, however, and now lives in semiretirement in Boca Raton, Florida.

LOBO

TYPE: *Monstrum legendarus minor lupus*

VARIANT NAME: Werewolf Boy

ORIGIN: Nerja, Spain

DESCRIPTION: 5 feet tall; half boy, half wolf

ABILITIES: skateboarding; playing video games; tormenting letter carriers

Discovered by LouLou & Tummie

ASSEMBLY INSTRUCTIONS

A Detach HEAD template. Curve chin and glue tabs 1–15 to gray areas 1–15.

B Detach RIGHT EAR template. Insert tab 16 into slot on top of right side of HEAD.

C Detach LEFT EAR template. Insert tab 17 into slot on top of left side of HEAD.

D Detach GLASSES template. Insert tabs 18–19 into slots on sides of HEAD.

E Detach RIGHT ARM and BODY templates. Insert tab 20 on RIGHT ARM into slot on right side of BODY and glue to gray area 20.

F Detach LEFT ARM template. Insert tab 21 on LEFT ARM into slot on left side of BODY and glue to gray area 21.

G Curve long section on BODY and glue tabs 22–34 to gray areas 22–34.

H Detach TAIL template. Insert tab 35 into slot on back of BODY.

I Detach LEGS template. Glue tabs 36–37 to gray areas 36–37.

J Glue tabs 38–41 on LEGS to gray areas 38–41 on BODY.

K Glue HEAD to BODY at gray area 42.

L Detach HAIR template. Insert tabs 43–44 into slots on top of HEAD.

O n the surface, Lobo appears to be an average 14-year-old boy, living with his perfectly normal family in a small village near Nerja, Spain—but when the moon is full, he transforms into a wolf monster. Just how this metamorphosis first came about is unknown. All Lobo knows is that one fateful night when he was 12 years old, he went out into the surrounding forest to search for his dog Marisco. His mother had warned him not to go because she could hear wolves baying in the distance, but Lobo was determined. When he didn't return after a few hours, Lobo's mother went looking for him. She found him curled up sound asleep in a nest of leaves, covered in mud. Lobo couldn't remember a thing about what had happened to him, but ever since then, in addition to transforming into a young wolf whenever there is a full moon, he has a strong dislike for mailmen and can't resist catching Frisbees with his mouth.

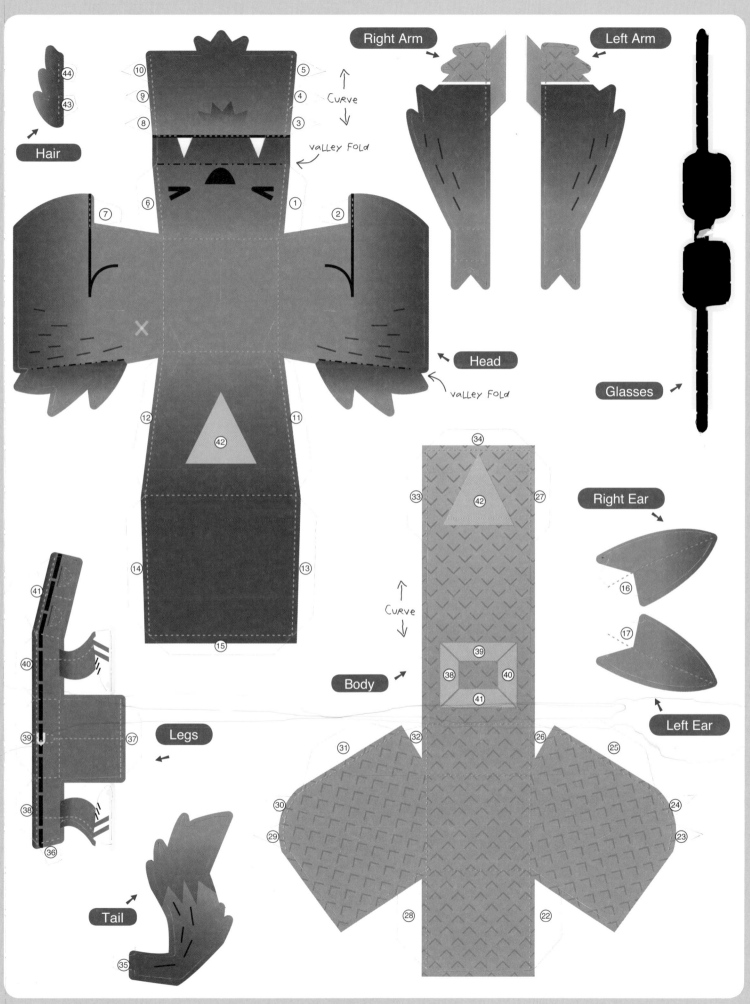

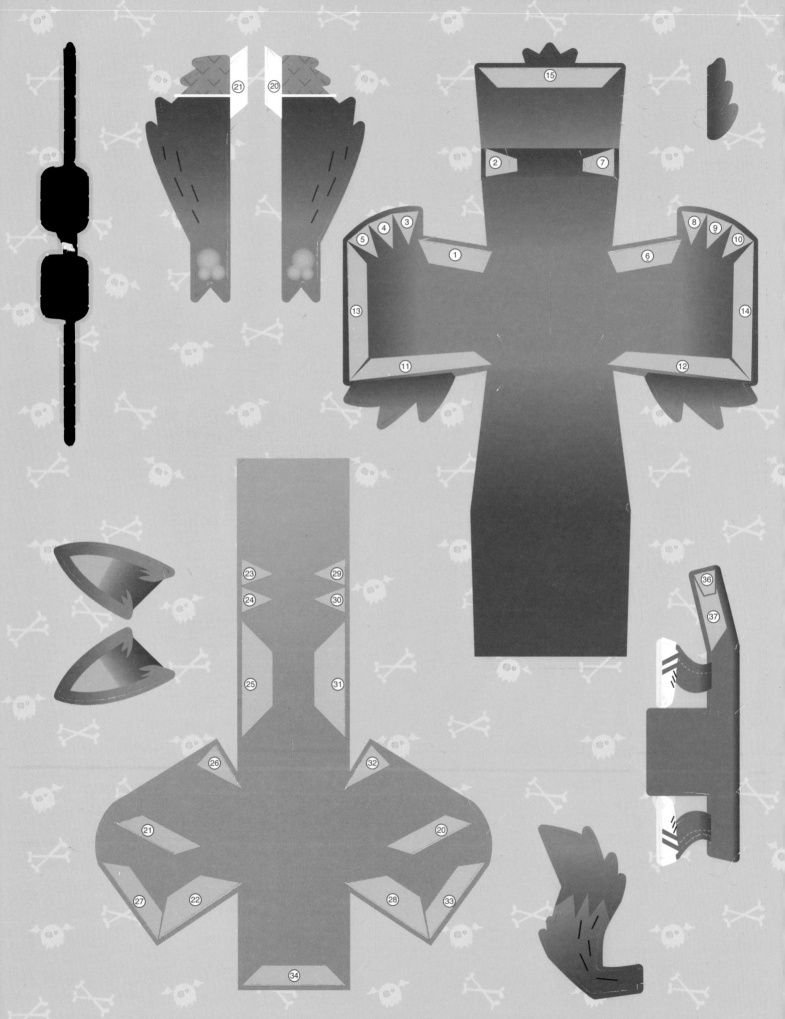

POLYPHEMUS

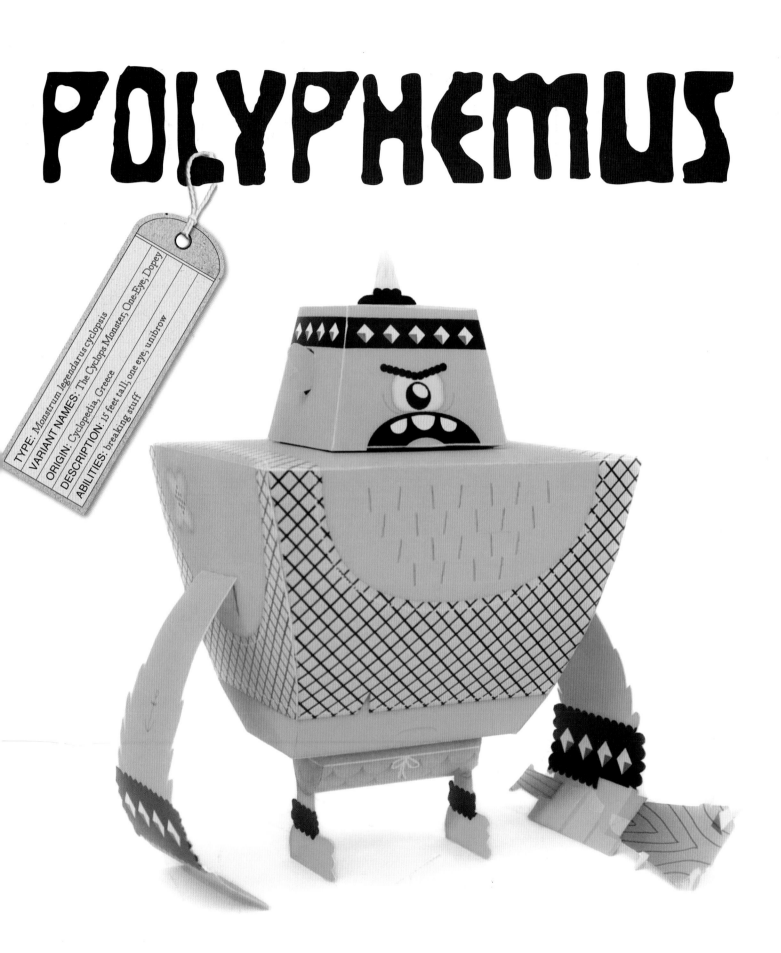

TYPE: Monstrum legendarus cyclopsis

VARIANT NAMES: The Cyclops Monster; One-Eye; Dopey

ORIGIN: Cyclopedia, Greece

DESCRIPTION: 15 feet tall, one eye, unibrow

ABILITIES: breaking stuff

POLYPHEMUS

Discovered by LouLou & Tummie

ASSEMBLY INSTRUCTIONS

A Detach BODY template. Glue tabs 1–19 to gray areas 1–19.

B Detach HEAD template. Remember to valley fold at ears so they stick out. Glue tabs 20–23 to gray areas 20–23.

C Detach HORN template. Insert tab 24 into slot on top of HEAD.

D Detach LEGS template. Curve large section around a pen or pencil and glue tabs 25–33 to gray areas 25–33.

E Detach RIGHT ARM template. Curve, and then glue tab 34 to gray area 34 on BODY.

F Detach LEFT ARM template. Curve, and then glue tab 35 to gray area 35 on BODY.

G Glue tabs 36–39 on HEAD to gray areas 36–39 on BODY.

H Glue LEGS to BODY at gray area 40.

This ancient one-eyed giant originally came from Cyclopedia in the Aegean Sea. He is almost five thousand years old, and very nearsighted, which makes him clumsy, so he often bumps into things when he walks. In addition to being rather lumbering and slow, he is not very smart—he basically doesn't do anything more than moan and groan all day and night. He has a giant wooden hammer that he swings quite often, but since he can't see very well, the hammer hardly ever hits its target. Instead of munching on people, which are his favorite treat, Polyphemus has to content himself with eating jellyfish that wash up on the beach where he lives.

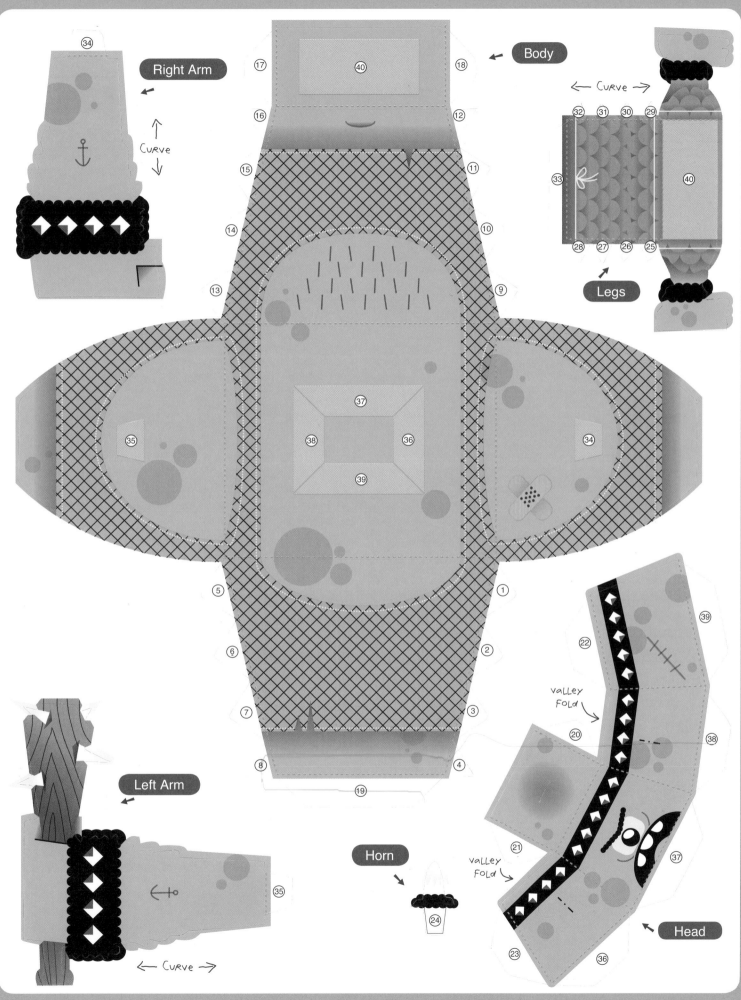

Right Arm

Curve

Body

Curve

Legs

Left Arm

Horn

Head

valley fold

valley fold

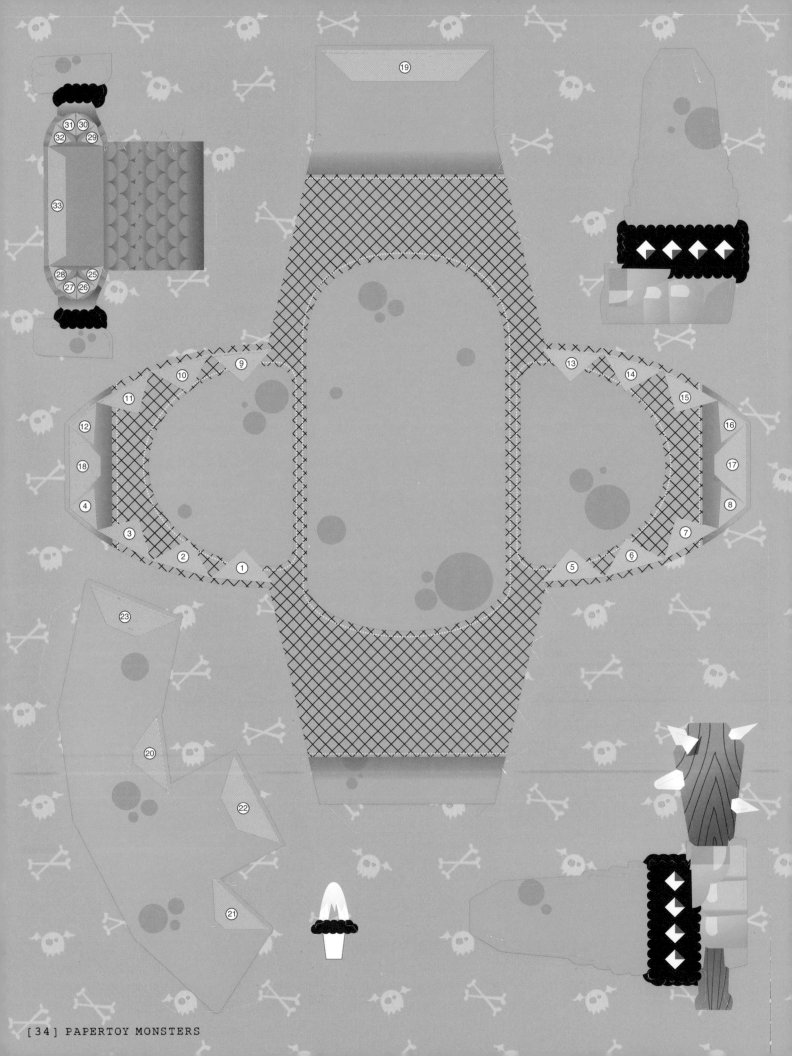

Li'l Vamp

TYPE: *Monstrum legendarus vampirus*

VARIANT NAMES: The Vampire Monster; Half Pint

ORIGIN: Transylvania

DESCRIPTION: 4 inches tall; large front teeth

ABILITIES: hunting birds; living forever; practicing tai chi

Li'l Vamp

Discovered by Christopher Bonnette

ASSEMBLY INSTRUCTIONS

A Detach HEAD template. Glue tabs 1–11 to gray areas 1–11.

B Detach EAR templates. Insert tab 12 into slot on right side of HEAD. Insert tab 13 into slot on left side of HEAD.

C Detach BODY template. Curve into a cone and glue tab 14 to gray area 14.

D Glue tabs 15–22 on BODY to gray areas 15–22 on HEAD.

E Detach RIGHT ARM and RIGHT HAND templates. Glue tabs 23–24 on RIGHT ARM to gray areas 23–24 on RIGHT HAND.

F Detach LEFT ARM and LEFT HAND templates. Glue tabs 25–26 on LEFT ARM to gray areas 25–26 on LEFT HAND.

G Glue RIGHT ARM to BODY at gray area 27.

H Glue LEFT ARM to BODY at gray area 28.

Li'l Vamp (a young cousin of Nosferatu) is a very tiny and very creepy vampire from Transylvania. Small as a rat, he uses an empty iPhone box as a coffin to shield himself from sunlight during the day. At night he wanders the countryside in search of waterbugs, slugs, and lizards. Sometimes he manages to hitch a ride on the back of a bat to hunt birds, which are his favorite meal. Stalking his prey from above, he will drop down on his unsuspecting victim and jam his two front teeth into its neck, draining it of all its blood. Li'l Vamp is relatively harmless to humans. An attack from this pint-size Dracula look-alike will leave behind a mosquito-like bite that itches for two months—irritating, but not lethal.

TYPE: *Monstrum legendarus frankenstein slothimus*

VARIANT NAMES: Frankenstein, Frank the Crank

ORIGIN: Slovenia

DESCRIPTION: 4 feet tall; favors green sneakers

ABILITIES: boring people into a coma

Discovered by Filippo Perin, aka PHIL

ASSEMBLY INSTRUCTIONS

A Detach HEAD and HEAD BOLT A–B templates. Insert tabs 1–2 on HEAD BOLT A into slots on left side of HEAD and glue to gray areas 1–2. Insert tabs 3–4 on HEAD BOLT B into slots on right side of HEAD and glue to gray areas 3–4.

B Glue tabs 5–8 on HEAD to gray areas 5–8.

C Detach BODY template. Glue tabs 9–12 to gray areas 9–12.

D Glue tabs 13–16 on BODY to gray areas 13–16 on inside of HEAD.

E Detach RIGHT SNEAKER template. Glue tabs 17–23 to gray areas 17–23.

F Detach LEFT SNEAKER template. Glue tabs 24–30 to gray areas 24–30.

G Detach RIGHT LEG and LEFT LEG templates. Curve into tubes and glue tabs 31 and 32 to gray areas 31 and 32.

H Insert RIGHT LEG and LEFT LEG tubes into star-shaped slots on top of SNEAKERS.

I Insert other end of RIGHT LEG and LEFT LEG tubes into star-shaped slots on front of BODY.

Little Frankie is the last descendant of a small family of monsters born from the brilliant mind of Dr. Frankenstein. Until recently, Frankie lived a relatively quiet life as a hip-hop star in a small village in Slovenia. A few years ago, however, his brain began to ooze an unknown toxic substance (thought to be the DNA of the original Frankenstein), and was replaced with the brain of a sloth. This makes Frankie exceptionally slow-witted and slow-moving. Due to the dullness of his mind, his raps are now extremely sluggish: One line can take him up to 13 hours to recite. It makes him a total bore. Frankie feeds on electricity, which sends sparks to his brain to keep his borrowed parts working.

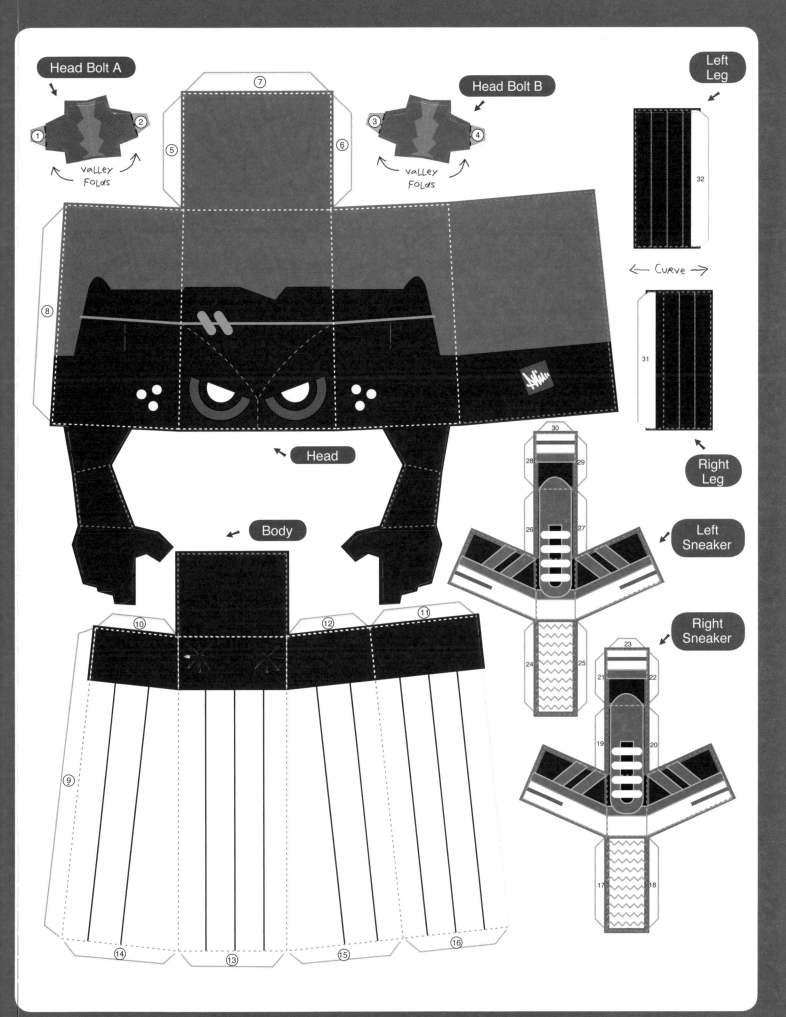

Head Bolt A

① ②

valley folds

Head Bolt B

③ ④

valley folds

⑦

⑤ ⑥

⑧

Head

Body

⑩ ⑫ ⑪

⑨

⑭ ⑬ ⑮ ⑯

Left Leg

32

← Curve →

31

Right Leg

Left Sneaker

30
28 29
26 27
24 25

Right Sneaker

23
21 22
19 20
17 18

TYPE: *Monstrum legendarus desertus yeticus*
VARIANT NAMES: Candy Beast; The Desert Yeti
ORIGIN: Earth's core
DESCRIPTION: 9 feet tall; purple-magenta color
ABILITIES: can smell chocolate across a 3,000-mile-wide desert; can build giant sand castles out of sand and saliva

Confetti Yeti

Discovered by Castleforte

ASSEMBLY INSTRUCTIONS

A Detach TONGUE and BODY templates. Glue tabs 1–2 on TONGUE to gray areas 1–2 on BODY.

B Glue tabs 3–26 on BODY to gray areas 3–26.

C Detach RIGHT ARM template. Glue tabs 27–37 to gray areas 27–37.

D Detach RIGHT FINGER template. Glue tabs 38–41 to gray areas 38–41.

E Glue tab 42 on RIGHT FINGER to gray area 42 on RIGHT ARM.

F Insert end of RIGHT ARM into horizontal slot on right side of BODY.

G Detach LEFT ARM template. Glue tabs 43–53 to gray areas 43–53.

H Detach LEFT FINGER template. Glue tabs 54–57 to gray areas 54–57.

I Glue tab 58 on LEFT FINGER to gray area 58 on LEFT ARM.

J Insert end of LEFT ARM into horizontal slot on left side of BODY.

K Detach HORNS templates. Insert tab 59 into vertical slot on left side of BODY and tab 60 into vertical slot on right side of BODY.

Confetti Yeti, also known as the Candy Beast, is said to have been born at the very center of the earth. Unlike his cousin, the more popular snow yeti, Confetti prefers to live where it is scorching hot. Last sighted in the desert near El Azizia, Libya, where it has been known to get as hot as 150°F, Confetti Yeti roams the sands in search of meteorites that have fallen to Earth. These he collects to trade with Bedouins, who give him candy in exchange for the meteorites (which they sell for thousands of dollars to scientists across the world). It's not exactly a fair trade for Confetti Yeti, but it's the only way he can get his paws on enough treats to feed his hyperactive sweet tooth. All that sugar makes him quite grumpy, of course—as sugar often does—so Confetti lives in a perpetual rage.

PHARAOH Thoth Amon

TYPE: *Monstrum legendarus mummiculus*

VARIANT NAMES: The Mummy; Amon the Invincible

ORIGIN: Valley of the Kings, Egypt

DESCRIPTION: 6 feet tall; covered with dirty linen scraps

ABILITIES: superhuman strength; dark magic

PHARAOH
Thoth Amon

Discovered by Scott Schaller

ASSEMBLY INSTRUCTIONS

A Detach SARCOPHAGUS template. Curve section with picture of mummy and glue tabs 1–16 to gray areas 1–16.

B Detach BODY template. Curve, and then glue tab 17 to gray area 17.

C Detach HEAD template. Insert tabs 18–19 on BODY into slots on bottom of HEAD and glue to gray areas 18–19.

D Glue tabs 20–26 on HEAD to gray areas 20–26.

E Detach RIGHT LEG template. Glue tab 27 to gray area 27 on inside of BODY.

F Detach LEFT LEG template. Glue tab 28 to gray area 28 on inside of BODY.

G Detach LEFT ARM template. Glue to BODY at gray area 29.

H Detach RIGHT ARM template. Glue to BODY at gray area 30.

I The Pharaoh can fit inside his sarcophagus if you curve his arms and fold up his knees.

Five thousand years ago, Pharaoh Thoth Amon ruled ancient Egypt with an iron fist and a cruel temperament. Like many pharaohs, Thoth was obsessed by the possibility of an afterlife and he spent many years studying the dark, secret magic of mummification. One evening, while practicing a resurrection spell, he made a slight miscalculation in the amount of liquified sand he needed to use, and he died as a result—or so it seemed. The truth is that the resurrection spell had partially worked, so when his tomb was uncovered by grave robbers some 4,500 years later, Thoth rose from his coffin. He didn't look or smell too nice, of course, and quickly set upon the grave robbers who had desecrated his tomb. Now he roams the desert searching for easy human prey to satisfy his need for life energy, hoping that one day he will return to some semblance of who he used to be.

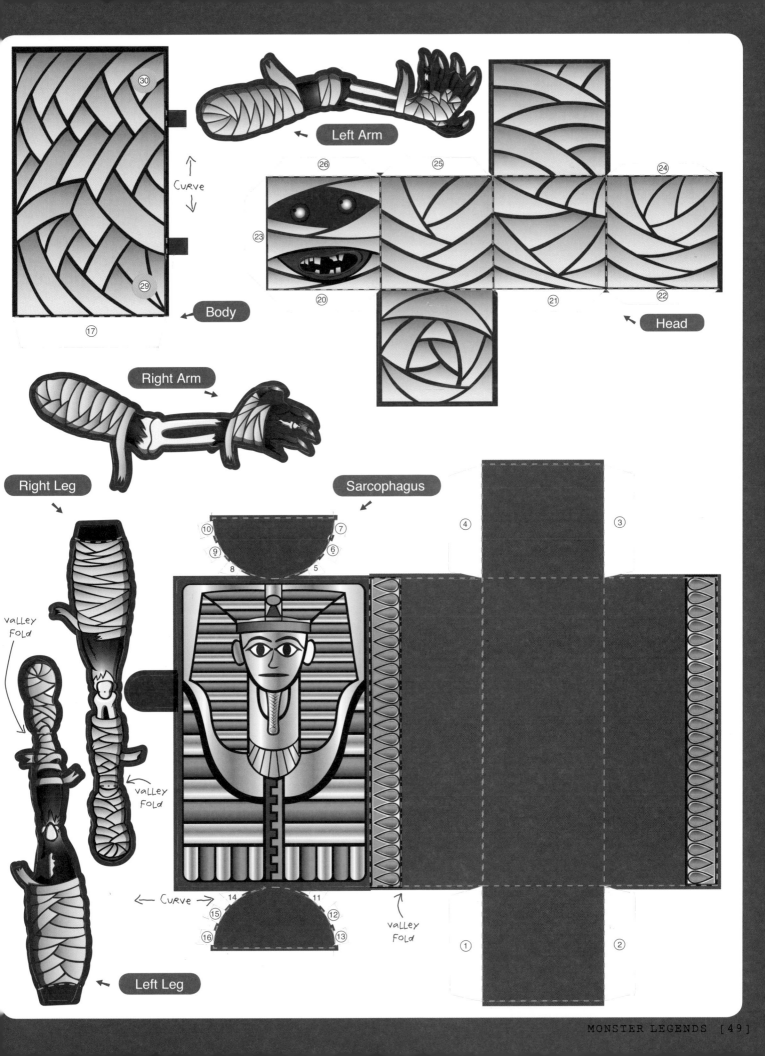

Left Arm

Curve

Body

Right Arm

Right Leg

Sarcophagus

valley fold

valley fold

valley fold

Curve

valley fold

Left Leg

Head

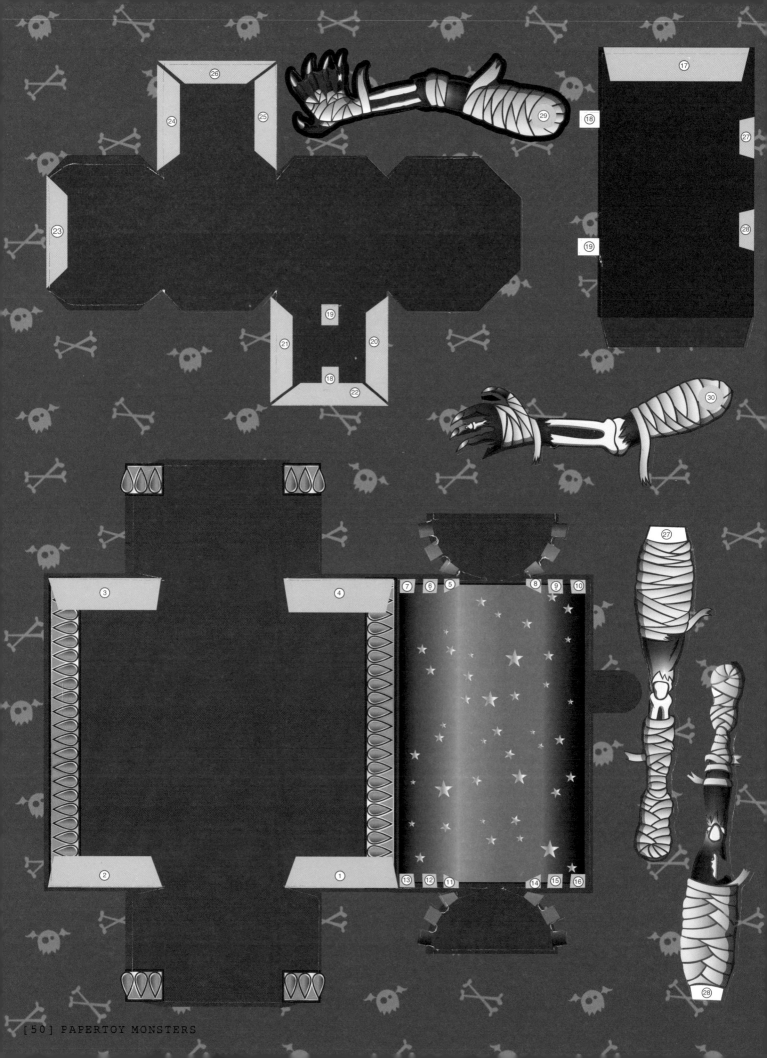

Cassandra

TYPE: Monstrum legendarus skeletonicus

VARIANT NAMES: The Skeleton Monster, Model Monster

ORIGIN: Mexico City, Mexico

DESCRIPTION: 6 feet tall; super thin

ABILITIES: great dresser; can strike a pose

CassandrA

Discovered by Bryan Rollins

ASSEMBLY INSTRUCTIONS

A Detach BODY template. Glue tabs 1–10 to gray areas 1–10.

B Detach RIGHT ARM template. Glue to BODY at gray area 11.

C Detach LEFT ARM template. Glue to BODY at gray area 12.

D Detach HEAD template. Curve face and glue tabs 13–16 to gray areas 13–16.

E Detach RIGHT EARRING and LEFT EARRING templates. Glue to HEAD at gray areas 17 and 18.

F Detach PONCHO template. Curve large section and glue tabs 19–20 to gray areas 19–20.

G Detach RIGHT LEG template. Curve into a tube and glue tabs 21–22 to gray areas 21–22.

H Detach LEFT LEG template. Curve into a tube and glue tabs 23–24 to gray areas 23–24.

I Insert tabs 25–27 on RIGHT LEG into slots 25–27 on bottom of BODY.

J Insert tabs 28–30 on LEFT LEG into slots 28–30 on bottom of BODY.

K Place PONCHO over BODY and rest it on shoulders.

L Insert tab 31 on HEAD into slot on top of BODY.

The soul of Cassandra Maria Catrina roams the busy metropolitan areas of Mexico City in the form of a skeleton monster. Born—or rather, reborn—at a Day of the Dead festival in Acapulco, Cassandra moved to the big city in order to be closer to her living relatives and to pursue a career in modeling. Stubborn and very snooty, Cassandra has a love for the finer things in life—or rather, death—and no tolerance for anything less. Her belief is that just because you have no skin, it doesn't mean you can't look fabulous.

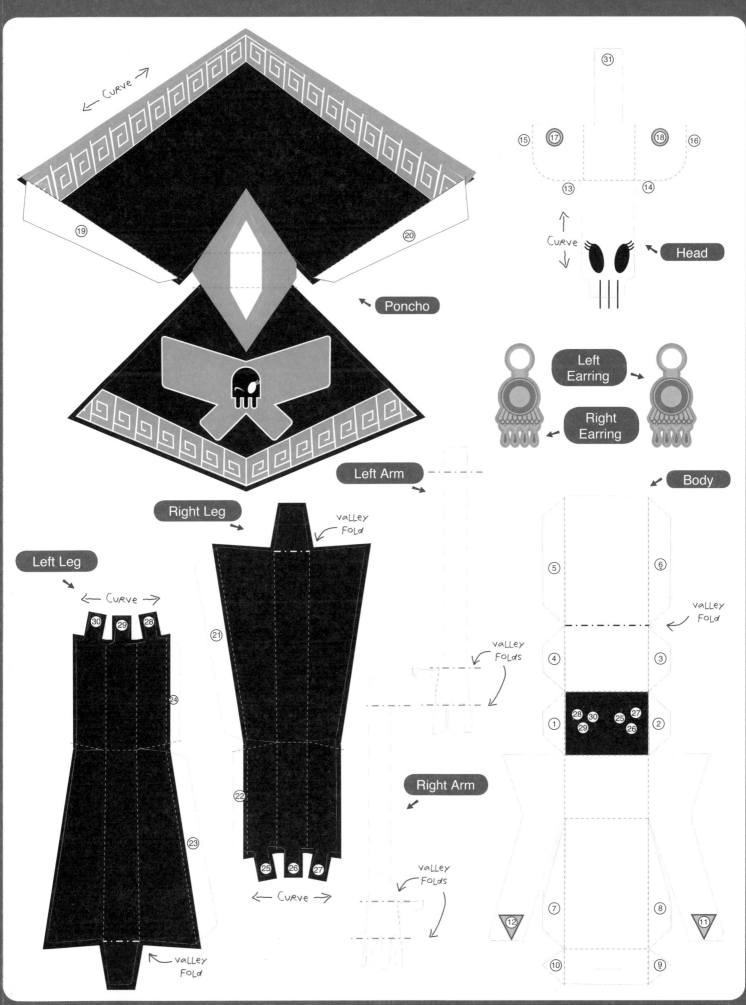

Poncho

Head

Left Earring

Right Earring

Body

Left Arm

Right Leg

Right Arm

Left Leg

MONSTER LEGENDS [53]

Zumbie

TYPE: *Monstrum legendarus zombicus*

VARIANT NAMES: The Zombie Monster; Lucky

ORIGIN: Mandeville, Jamaica

DESCRIPTION: 5 feet tall; unnaturally long arms

ABILITIES: excels at math; incredibly green thumbs (can grow yams anywhere he pleases)

Zumbie

Discovered by Bryan Rollins

ASSEMBLY INSTRUCTIONS

A Detach HEAD template. Curve front and back and glue tabs 1–9 to gray areas 1–9.

B Detach PONYTAIL template. Insert tab 10 into upper slot on back of HEAD.

C Detach BODY template. Glue tabs 11–17 to gray areas 11–17.

D Detach RIGHT ARM template. Glue to BODY at gray area 18.

E Detach LEFT ARM template. Glue to BODY at gray area 19.

F Detach NECK template. Insert tab 20 into slot on front of BODY.

G Insert tab 21 on NECK into lower slot on back of HEAD.

Zumbie is a hermit zombie monster from the lush Mandeville highlands in Jamaica. He died under a full moon at the age of 81, at 8:01 P.M., on 8/1/1881. No one knows the significance of this strange and rare event, but something mystical must have happened that night because exactly 81 days later, on 10/21 (10 minus 2 equals 8; add a 1 and you get 81), Zumbie rose from the dead to walk the earth again. It is believed that during his life Zumbie must have been something of a recluse, since he continues that tradition in his death: He keeps to himself until he gets hungry and runs out of yams, the one and only human food he'll still eat. He prefers not to feed on the brains of tourists, which so many of the other zombies favor, because even though they are quite tasty, doing this would mean he has to be seen. To a hermit zombie, being in public is the worst thing in the world that can happen to you (unless you happen to have died on your 81st birthday at 8:01 P.M. on August 1, 1881).

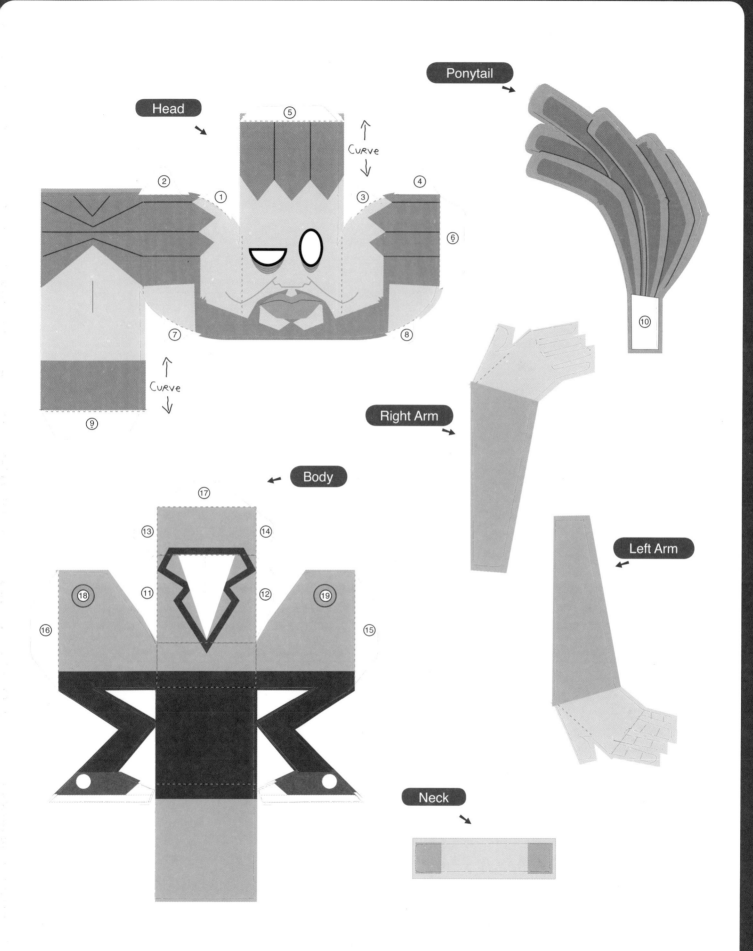

Head

⑤

Curve

② ① ③ ④

⑥

⑦ ⑧

Curve

⑨

Ponytail

⑩

Right Arm

Body

⑰

⑬ ⑭

⑪ ⑫

⑱ ⑲

⑯ ⑮

Left Arm

Neck

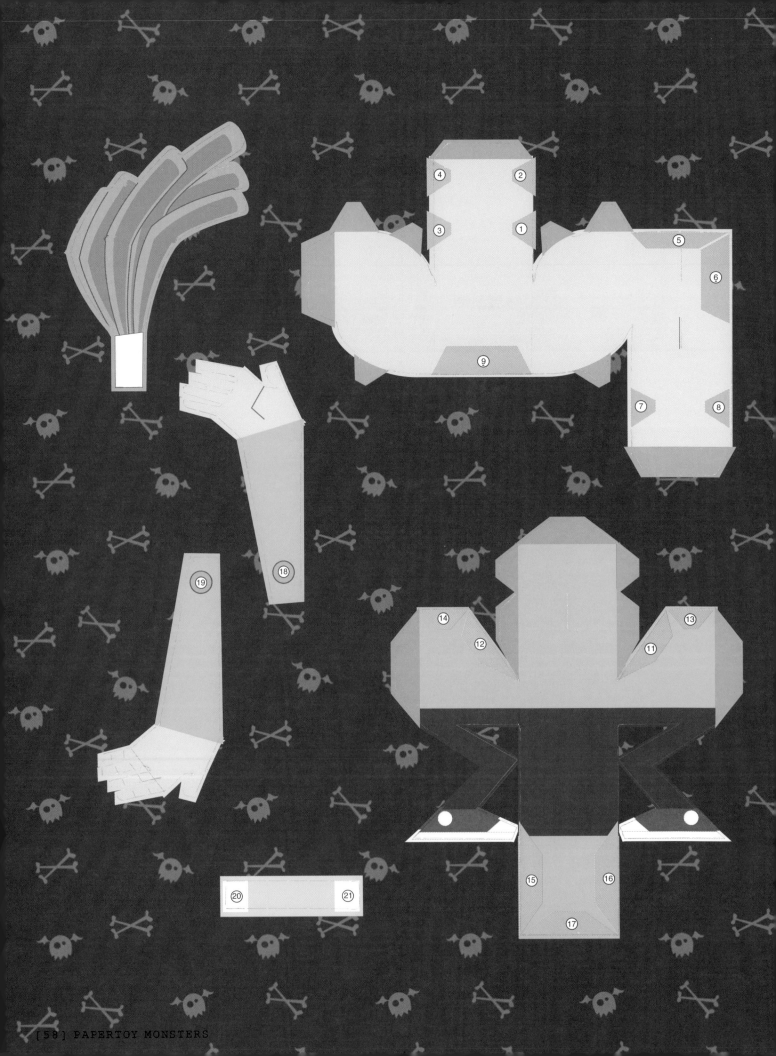

EARTH, OCEAN & SPACE MONSTERS

gene chemzyme

TYPE: *Monstrum extraterrestrialis chemzymicus*

VARIANT NAME: The Creature from the Deep

ORIGIN: outer space/ocean depths

DESCRIPTION: 15-20 feet long; six tentacles plus long spiked tail; covered with scales

ABILITIES: strong swimmer; card shark

Gene Chemzyme

Discovered by Marko Zubak

ASSEMBLY INSTRUCTIONS

A Detach BODY template. Glue tab 1 to gray area 1.

B Curve head and glue tabs 2–3 to gray areas 2–3.

This monster literally sprang out of the depths of the ocean. Thought to be a mutation of a space creature that fell to Earth during a South African nuclear testing experiment in the Indian Ocean, Gene Chemzyme first surfaced on a beach during a surfing competition. After frightened beachcombers mistook him for some kind of primitive shark and threw an assortment of rocks and conch shells at him, Gene disappeared into the ocean for several decades. There he grew to his current formidable size. Rarely does he make an appearance on the world stage, preferring to live in the abyssal plains at the bottom of the ocean, which must remind him of outer space.

SQUIDBEAK

TYPE: Monstrum oceanus squidicus

VARIANT NAMES: The Giant Squid, Electro Squid

ORIGIN: Gulf of Oman

DESCRIPTION: 50 feet long with tentacles outstretched

ABILITIES: zapping enemies into oblivion, bodysurfing

SQUIDBEAK

Discovered by Matthijs Kamstra, aka [mck]

ASSEMBLY INSTRUCTIONS

A Detach BODY template. Curve into a tube and glue tabs 1–12 to gray areas 1–12.

B Detach BASE template. Curve into a tube and glue tab 13 to gray area 13.

C Glue gray area 14 on BASE to gray area 14 on inside of BODY.

D Detach TENTACLE A template. Glue tabs 15–16 to gray areas 15–16. Glue tabs 17–18 to gray areas 17–18 on BODY. Curve tentacle up.

E Detach TENTACLE B template. Glue tabs 19–20 to gray areas 19–20. Glue tabs 21–22 to gray areas 21–22 on BODY. Curve tentacle up.

F Detach TENTACLE C template. Glue tabs 23–24 to gray areas 23–24. Glue tabs 25–26 to gray areas 25–26 on BODY. Curve tentacle up.

G Detach BEAK A template. Glue tab 27 to gray area 27. Glue tabs 28–31 to gray areas 28–31 on BODY.

H Detach BEAK B template. Glue tab 32 to gray area 32. Glue tabs 33–36 to gray areas 33–36 on BODY.

I Detach BEAK C template. Glue tab 37 to gray area 37. Glue tabs 38–41 to gray areas 38–41 on BODY.

Slimy, fierce, and humongous, Squidbeak was born deep inside the wreckage of the SS *Galvani*, a supersecret industrial submarine. The crew was conducting experiments on the effects of gamma rays on marine life when their sub went down during a lightning storm over the Gulf of Oman. The last known communiqué between the ship's scientists and the corporation funding its research was cryptic: "Help us! The beaker . . . the lightning . . . it's alive!" These words were followed by spine-chilling human screams and what sounded like a screeching cat, which many believe to be the sound of Squidbeak attacking its human makers. Although rarely seen, Squidbeak is known to live in the warm waters of the Arabian Sea.

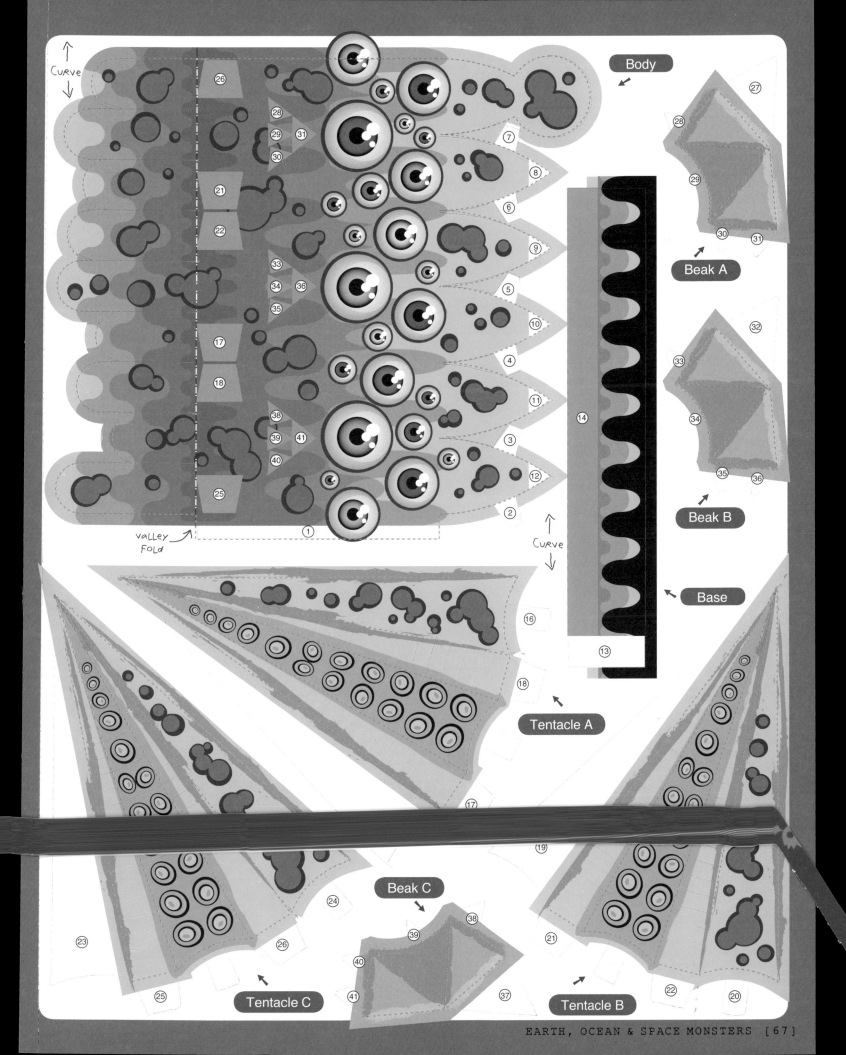

Curve

Body

27

26

28

29 31

28

21

29

22

Beak A

30 31

33

34 36

32

35

17

33

18

34

38

39 41

40

35 36

25

Beak B

14

1

2

Curve

16

13

Base

valley
FOLD

18

Tentacle A

17

19

Beak C

24

38

26

39

23

40

21

25

Tentacle C

41

37

Tentacle B

22

20

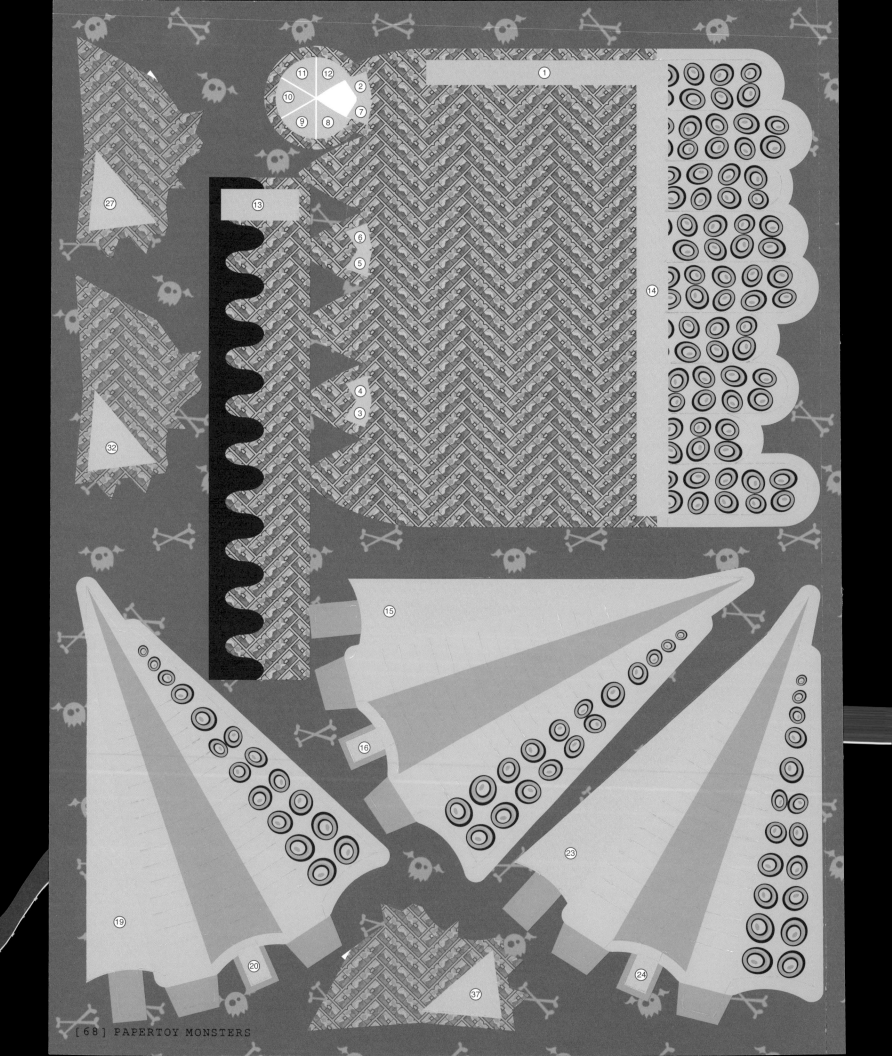

OctoPup

TYPE: *Monstrum oceanus octopi*

VARIANT NAMES: The Sea Monster, Li'l Octo

ORIGIN: the Mariana Trench at the bottom of the sea

DESCRIPTION: 25 feet tall; eight tentacles; big ears

ABILITIES: great at fetch; tap dance prodigy; good swimmer

OctoPup

Discovered by Rememberthelittleguy

ASSEMBLY INSTRUCTIONS

A Detach BODY template. Glue tabs 1–4 to gray areas 1–4.

B Detach TENTACLE A–H templates. Curve them upward and glue tabs 5–12 to gray areas 5–12 on inside of BODY.

C Detach HEAD template. Glue tabs 13–17 to gray areas 13–17.

D Glue gray area 18 on inside of HEAD to gray area 18 on BODY.

Unlike Squidbeak, who was the rather unnatural consequence of failed laboratory experiments conducted by humans, OctoPup is a biologically natural, previously unknown sea monster born in the deepest part of the Pacific Ocean. Only 4 years old, OctoPup is already over 25 feet tall, and will soon be large enough to eat entire cargo ships in a single gulp. Just like his father before him, who is said to be responsible for the disappearance of more than 40 vessels over the centuries, OctoPup is already known to have eaten about a dozen smaller boats. The good news is, unlike his father, OctoPup doesn't eat people, so he always spits out the passengers before he digests the boats.

Abagon

TYPE: *Monstrum terrestrialis dragonicus*

VARIANT NAMES: The Dragon Monster; The Boraboran

ORIGIN: French Polynesia

DESCRIPTION: 30 feet tall; orange skin, green horns; cute furry patch atop head

ABILITIES: breathing fire; barbecue chef extraordinaire

Abagon

Discovered by Tetsuya Watabe

ASSEMBLY INSTRUCTIONS

A Detach HEAD template. Glue tabs 1–8 to gray areas 1–8.

B Detach CROWN template. Glue to HEAD at gray areas 9–10.

C Detach LEFT FOOT template. Curve, and then glue tab 11 to gray area 11.

D Detach RIGHT FOOT template. Curve, and then glue tab 12 to gray area 12.

E Detach BODY template. Glue tabs 13–14 to gray areas 13–14.

F Glue tab 15 on LEFT FOOT to gray area 15 on BODY. Glue tab 16 on BODY to gray area 16 on LEFT FOOT.

G Glue tab 17 on RIGHT FOOT to gray area 17 on BODY. Glue tab 18 on BODY to gray area 18 on RIGHT FOOT.

H Glue tabs 19–20 on BODY to gray areas 19–20.

I Detach NECK template. Glue tabs 21–24 to gray areas 21–24.

J Glue tab 25 on NECK to gray area 25 on BODY. Glue tab 26 on NECK to gray area 26 on HEAD.

K Detach TAIL template. Glue tabs 27–28 on BODY to gray areas 27–28 on TAIL.

A humongous dragon monster from Tahiti, this 320-year-old female is still so young for her kind that her wings are not yet fully developed. When they finally do sprout—about 500 years from now—Abagon will be able to fly six times faster than the speed of sound. At the moment, she spends much of her time napping near an active volcano in Bora-Bora, where she feeds on the thousands of coral fish that live in the lagoon. She enjoys hunting for sharks, too, which the local Polynesians love because it allows them to dive deep into the waters for precious black pearls without fear of a shark attack.

Zumolla

TYPE: *Monstrum oceanus crustaceous*

VARIANT NAMES: The Sea Beast, Megaclaw

ORIGIN: Monster Island, South China Sea

DESCRIPTION: 22 feet tall; blue skin; two pincers

ABILITIES: can dive to depths of 4,000 feet; champion synchronized swimmer

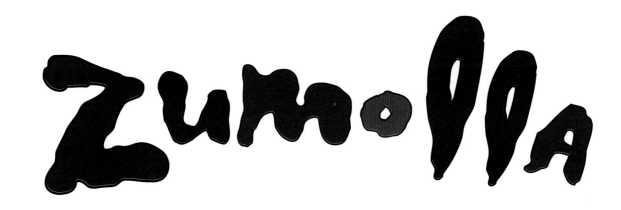

Discovered by Tetsuya Watabe

ASSEMBLY INSTRUCTIONS

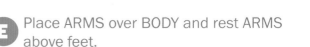

A Detach HEAD template. Glue tabs 1–4 to gray areas 1–4.

B Detach BODY template. Glue tab 5 to gray area 5.

C Detach ARMS template. Curve, and then glue tabs 6–9 to gray areas 6–9.

D Detach CHEST template. Glue tabs 10–11 on CHEST.

E Place ARMS over BODY and rest ARMS above feet.

F Glue gray area 14 on inside of HEAD to gray area 14 on BODY.

This large sea creature was born on Monster Island, a place rumored to be in the South China Sea (though no one knows for sure). With razor-sharp pincers and a tough exoskeleton, Zumolla has been spotted in many locations all across the globe. When he is not submerged in water as deep as 4,000 feet, he can usually be found belly-surfing near the hottest beaches—from the south of France to southern California. Although generally peaceful, Zumolla is responsible for the accidental sinking of seven luxury yachts in the Mediterranean.

ZOGG!

TYPE: *Monstrum extraterrestrialis farticus*

VARIANT NAME: The Farting Spaceman

ORIGIN: *Zondor 38Q*

DESCRIPTION: 7 feet wide; one eye; greenish-blue skin

ABILITIES: belching acid; sonic farting; eating expired food

Discovered by Josh McKible

ASSEMBLY INSTRUCTIONS

A Detach BODY and TONGUE templates. Glue TONGUE to BODY at gray area 1.

B Glue tabs 2–6 on BODY to gray areas 2–6.

C Detach TENTACLE A–D templates. Glue tabs 7–10 to gray areas 7–10 on BODY.

D Detach CAT FOOD templates. Keep them loose or glue them inside Zogg!'s mouth or onto his tentacles and body.

Zogg! is an alien from the planet Zondor 38Q. A disgusting creature that belches acid and farts at an extremely high pitch, Zogg! will eat anything he can get his tentacles on (his favorite meal is canned cat food). Not much else is known about Zogg! While some scientists speculate that his belches and farts are a form of coded language that should be studied, all attempts at communication have ended in failure because no one can endure getting too close to the alien. While not considered dangerous to humans, Zogg!'s odor is toxic if inhaled for extended periods of time and the force of his farts has caused temporary deafness in more than one stubborn alienologist. Prolonged contact—even in the name of science—is discouraged.

THE X FROM OUTER SPACE

TYPE: *Monstrum extraterrestrialis exxus*

VARIANT NAME: The Thing from Outer Space

ORIGIN: an unknown galaxy

DESCRIPTION: legs made of metal; exposed pink brain

ABILITIES: can use his three eyes to brainwash victims; accomplished pastry chef

THE X FROM OUTER SPACE

Discovered by Dolly Oblong

ASSEMBLY INSTRUCTIONS

A Detach HEAD template. Glue tabs 1–11 to gray areas 1–11.

B Detach TOE A and FOOT A templates. Curve TOE A into a circle. Glue tabs 12–23 on FOOT A to gray areas 12–23 on TOE A. Glue tab 24 on TOE A to gray area 24.

C Detach TOE B and FOOT B templates. Curve TOE B into a circle. Glue tabs 25–36 on FOOT B to gray areas 25–36 on TOE B. Glue

D TOE C into a circle. Glue tabs 38–49 on FOOT C to gray areas 38–49 on TOE C. Glue tab 50 on TOE C to gray area 50.

E Detach ANKLE A–C and LEG A–C templates. Insert slots on bottom of LEGS A–C into slots on top of ANKLES A–C.

F Insert tabs 51–54 on LEG A and ANKLE A into slots on top of FOOT A. Insert tabs 55–58 on LEG B and ANKLE B into slots on top of FOOT B. Insert tabs 59–62 on LEG C and ANKLE C into slots on top of FOOT C.

G Insert tabs 63–65 on leg pieces into slots

The galaxy The X from Outer Space originally came from is unknown. After landing his spaceship in the Sea of Japan, he spent the first few years trying to conquer Earth by hostile means. When that failed, he decided to learn Japanese and take up permanent residence in Tokyo. There he was recruited by the Japanese government to work on top-secret research about alien life-forms. In his spare time, X collects toy robots and models from famous Japanese manga artists. Although he appears, at the moment, to be a responsible citizen of Earth, X still harbors a deep animosity for humans and a secret desire to rule the world. Using his cute appearance as a cover, X has mastered the art of brainwashing (he uses his eyes to hypnotize his victims) and plans to build an army of brainwashed followers to aid in his evil campaign for world domination.

MEGA LARB

TYPE: *Monstrum extraterrestrialis larbus*

VARIANT NAMES: The Mega Monster; Pepto Abysmal

ORIGIN: outer space, planet unknown

DESCRIPTION: 22 feet tall, pink, furry

ABILITIES: practically invulnerable to Earth weapons; excellent babysitter

MEGA LARB

Discovered by Christopher Bonnette

ASSEMBLY INSTRUCTIONS

A Detach BODY template. Glue tabs 1–15 to gray areas 1–15.

B Detach RIGHT HORN template. Glue tab 16 to gray area 16. Glue tabs 17–20 to gray areas 17–20 on BODY.

C Detach LEFT HORN template. Glue tab 21 to gray area 21. Glue tabs 22–25 to gray

D slot on back of BODY.

E Detach RIGHT ARM template. Insert tab 27 into slot on right side of BODY.

F Detach LEFT ARM template. Insert tab 28 into slot on left side of BODY.

G Detach RIGHT LEG template. Glue tab 29 to gray area 29.

H Detach RIGHT FOOT template. Glue tabs 30–32 to gray areas 30–32 on RIGHT LEG.

I Detach LEFT LEG template. Glue tab 33 to gray area 33.

J Detach LEFT FOOT template. Glue tabs

K Insert top of RIGHT LEG into square-shaped opening on bottom of BODY on right side. Insert top of LEFT LEG into square-shaped opening on bottom of BODY on left side.

Mega Larb is a giant alien monster from well beyond the Milky Way galaxy. No one has any idea how or why he got to Earth—people only know that he appeared one day outside a small suburb in present-day St. Petersburg (then known as Leningrad). After seven months of failed military strikes against the giant monster, with virtually no effect at all, the Soviet government finally decided that destroying the creature was unnecessary. It turns out that Mega Larb is a very mellow fellow. He shows aggression only when provoked, and he is very mindful of his surroundings. Currently residing off the coast of Florida, where he spends most of his time in the water, Mega Larb loves to entertain young children by doing backflips, wrangling sharks, and blowing giant saltwater bubbles.

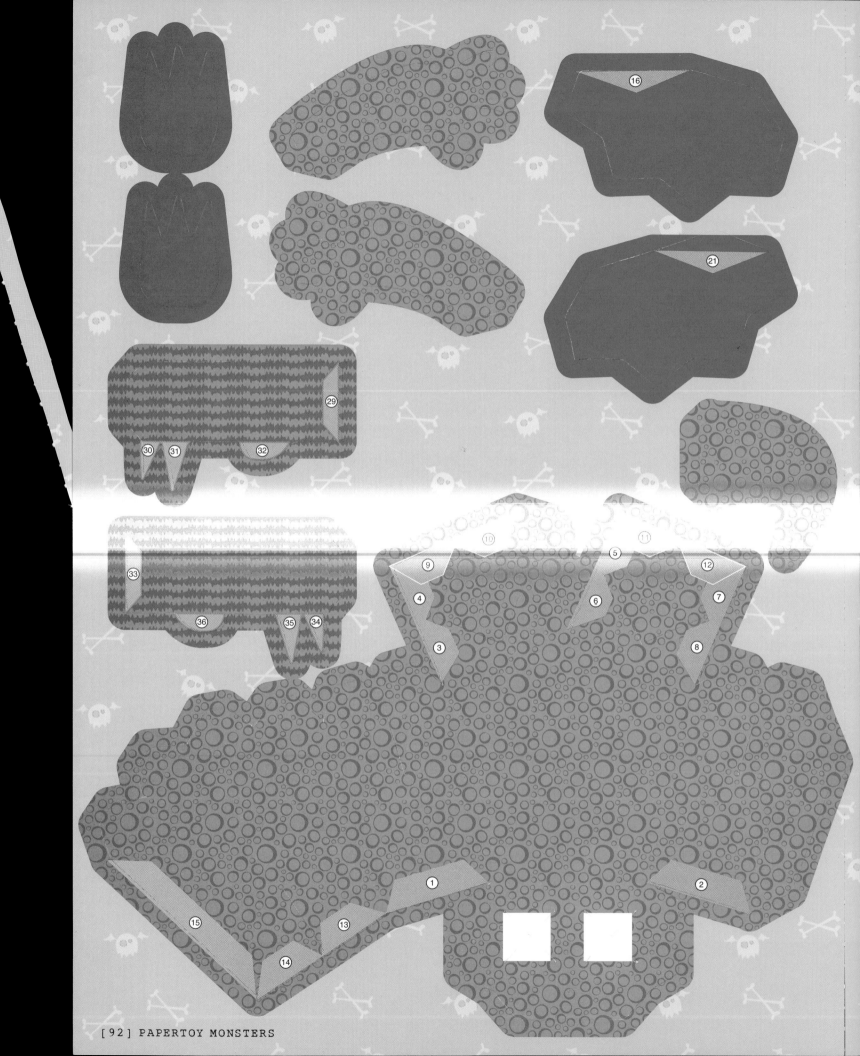

ZWART

TYPE: *Monstrum extraterrestrialis blackholicus*
VARIANT NAMES: The Monster in the Shadows;
The Shadow Lurker
ORIGIN: a black hole
DESCRIPTION: amorphous; gaslike; dark; big or small
ABILITIES: shape-shifting; alchemy

ZWART

Discovered by 3EyedBear

ASSEMBLY INSTRUCTIONS

A Detach BODY template. Glue tabs 1–11 to gray areas 1–11.

B Glue tab 12 to gray area 12.

C Insert slot 13 into slot 14 behind Zwart.

D Glue BODY together at gray area 15.

Zwart is one of the most ancient monsters in existence—going back billions of years to the very beginning of the universe. Born inside a black hole, Zwart consists of nothing but pure dark matter. He can change shapes at will, shrink to the size of an atom or become large enough to eclipse the moon. Often found lurking behind humans, Zwart feeds on the subatomic particles in them. Although he hates light, it is the very thing that defines him: The stronger the light, the stronger he becomes. Young humans—and adults who retain their ability to believe in things they can't see or touch—can catch glimpses of Zwart during solar eclipses.

VALLEY FOLD

valley folds

Body

Make sure you fold his interior tabs to let light through

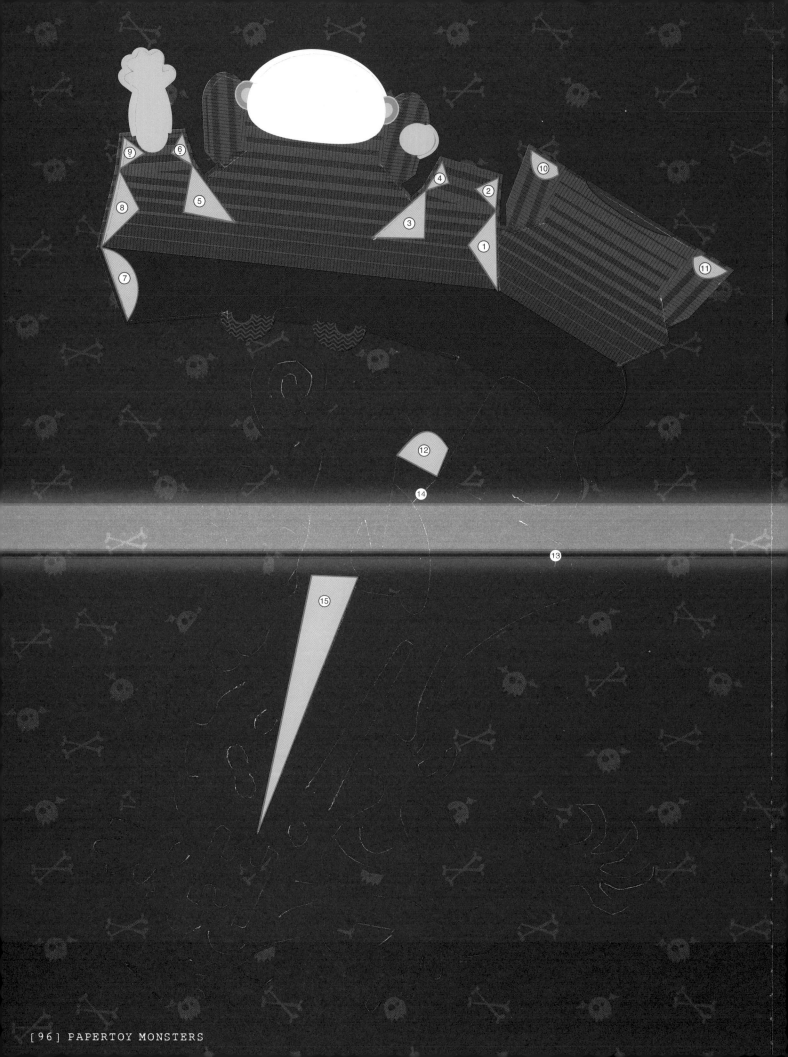

Scorpion Robot

TYPE: *Monstrum extraterrestrialis roboticus*

VARIANT NAME: The Robot Monster

ORIGIN: outer space; an unknown desertlike planet

DESCRIPTION: 10 feet across; six legs and two pincers

ABILITIES: destroying everything in its path; accomplished pianist

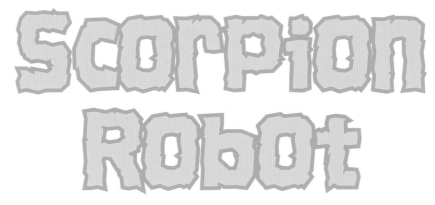

Scorpion Robot

Discovered by Matthijs Kamstra, aka [mck]

ASSEMBLY INSTRUCTIONS

A Detach RIGHT ARM template. Glue tabs 1–2 to gray areas 1–2.

B Detach LEFT ARM template. Glue tabs 3–4 to gray areas 3–4.

C Detach RIGHT HAND template. Glue tabs 5–8 to gray areas 5–8.

D Detach LEFT HAND template. Glue tabs

E

F Glue LEFT HAND to LEFT ARM at gray area 14.

G Detach LEGS templates. Glue tabs 15–20 to gray areas 15–20.

H Detach HEAD template. Glue tabs 21–25 to gray areas 21–25.

I Detach BODY template. Glue tabs 26–33 to gray areas 26–33.

J Insert LEGS into triangular openings on BODY so that gray areas 34–39 on LEGS meet with gray areas 34–39 on BODY, but do not glue yet.

K Insert HEAD into triangular opening on top of BODY. Glue HEAD to BODY at gray areas 40–42.

L Note that gray areas 34–39 on LEGS and

BODY to gray areas 43–48 on BODY. Glue tab 49 on BODY to gray area 49.

M Insert LEFT ARM into triangular opening on left side of HEAD and glue gray area 50 on LEFT ARM to gray area 50 on inside of HEAD.

N Insert RIGHT ARM into triangular opening on right side of HEAD and glue gray area 51 on RIGHT ARM to gray area 51 on inside of HEAD.

This robotic menace from outer space shot through our atmosphere encased in a car-size asteroid that struck the earth in White Sands, New Mexico. Almost immediately upon impact, the alien robot spilled out of the wreckage and assumed the genetic makeup of the first terrestrial creature it encountered: a desert scorpion. After its biological host died, the robot morphed its own digital plasma into the DNA of the scorpion, creating a lethal blend of animal and machine. It is as big as a tank, and its pincers are capable of tearing through stone or steel without any difficulty. It eats machine parts for fuel, and has been known to down an entire field of windmills when hungry.

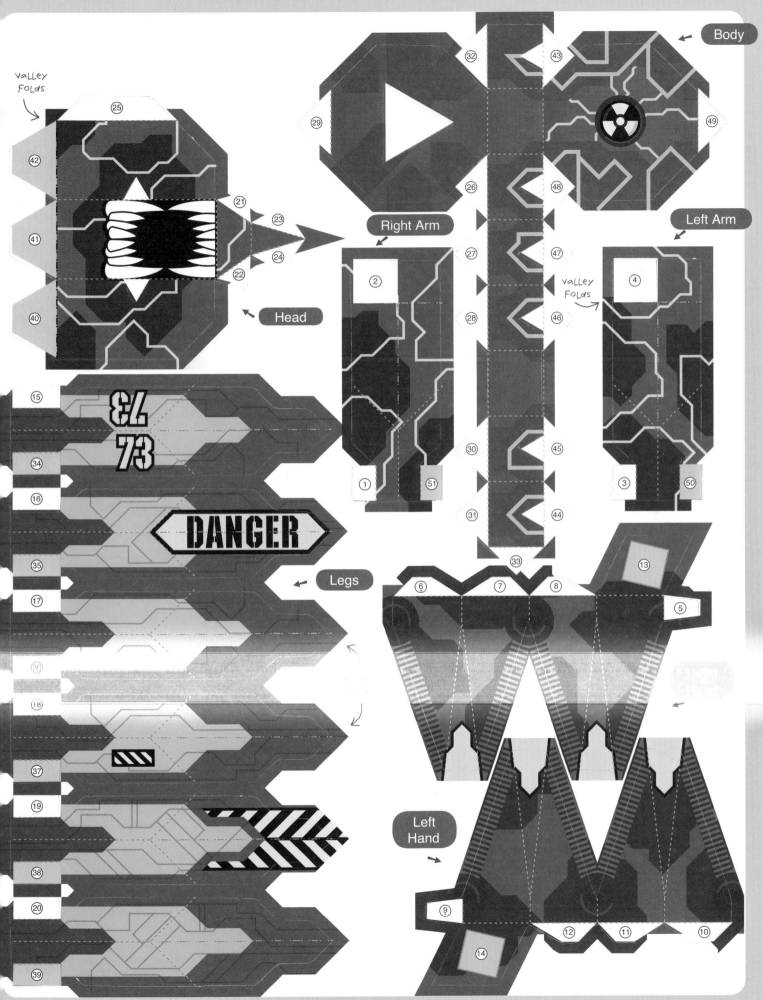

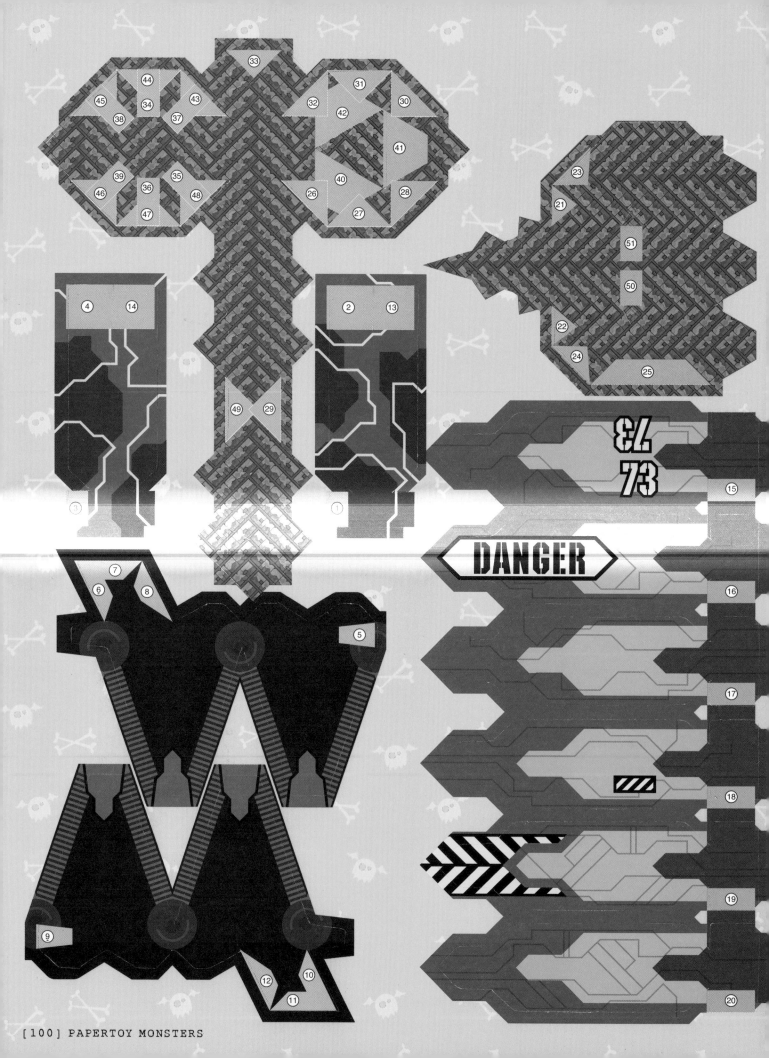

Daright

TYPE: *Monstrum extraterrestrialis angelicus demonicus*

VARIANT NAME: The Good and Evil Monster

ORIGIN: born where light and dark meet

DESCRIPTION: a shape shifter whose appearance changes

ABILITIES: can be in many places at the same time, can travel at the speed of light, can eat children's shadows

Daright

Discovered by Marko Zubak

ASSEMBLY INSTRUCTIONS

A Detach BODY template. Glue tab 1 to gray area 1. Curve head and glue tabs 2–5 to gray areas 2–5.

B Detach LEFT HAND and RIGHT HAND templates. Insert tabs 6–7 into slots on left and right sides of BODY.

Detach HORN template. Insert tab 8 into

Born where light and dark meet, this dragon-angel monster is a very unique creature. She can change her form from solid to gas and use her gaseous form to travel great distances across the universe at the speed of light. She can also bend light and shadow to her will. Caught in the perennial struggle between good and evil, Daright can choose her path at any time. When she is good, she is helpful and kind. When she chooses evil, she will wreak havoc on anyone who gets in her way. Part dragon, part angel, and all monster, Daright can also turn herself into binary code, thus enabling her to go anywhere in the universe instantaneously.

NISHWYNDYM

TYPE: *Monstrum terrestrialis amazonica*

VARIANT NAMES: The Tree Monster; Arbor-Eat'Em

ORIGIN: enchanted forest, Amazon Basin

DESCRIPTION: 100 feet tall; leafless; two arm limbs

ABILITIES: incredible strength; extraordinary wisdom; can play upwards of 53 xylophones simultaneously

NISHWYNDYM

Discovered by Jason Harlan

ASSEMBLY INSTRUCTIONS

A Detach BODY template. Glue tabs 1–6 to gray areas 1–6.

B Detach LEFT ARM template. Glue to BODY at gray area 7.

C Detach RIGHT ARM template. Glue to BODY at gray area 8.

This living tree monster hails from an enchanted forest deep inside the Amazonian jungle. Incredibly strong, impervious to pretty much everything but fire, Nishwyndym is wise beyond his 100,000 years, having seen the rise and fall of many species on Earth. He considers humans to be trivial in the grand scheme of things—they are spindly and rootless, reckless users of the earth. He will swallow any human who has the misfortune of straying into his territory—not out of hunger, since he's a vegetarian, but out of anger for what humans have done to his forests and jungles. Be warned: His bite is stronger than his bark.

Rockmon

TYPE: Monstrum terrestrialis rockabus
VARIANT NAMES: The Rock Monster, Mini Geo
ORIGIN: Red Rock Canyon, Nevada, U.S.A.
DESCRIPTION: 1 inch tall; looks like a pebble
ABILITIES: can blend into any rocky surface; champion hide-and-seeker

Discovered by Nana Pong, aka Roomism

ASSEMBLY INSTRUCTIONS

A Detach HEAD template. Glue tabs 1–2 to gray areas 1–2.

B Detach EARS template. Glue tabs 3–5 on HEAD to gray areas 3–5 on EARS. Glue tabs 6–15 on head piece to gray areas 6–15 to close.

C Detach RIGHT LEG OUTSIDE and RIGHT LEG EDGE A templates. Glue tabs 16–20 on RIGHT LEG EDGE A to gray areas 16–20 on RIGHT LEG OUTSIDE, including all unlabeled tabs and gray areas.

D Detach RIGHT LEG EDGE B template. Glue tab 21 on RIGHT LEG EDGE A to gray area 21 on RIGHT LEG EDGE B. Glue tabs 22–27 on RIGHT LEG EDGE B to gray areas 22–27 on right leg piece, including all unlabeled tabs and gray areas.

E Detach RIGHT LEG EDGE C template. Glue tab 28 on RIGHT LEG EDGE B to gray area 28 on RIGHT LEG EDGE C. Glue tabs 29–34 to gray areas 29–34 on right leg piece, including all unlabeled tabs and gray areas.

F Detach RIGHT LEG INSIDE template. Glue tabs 35–50 on right leg piece to gray areas 35–50 on RIGHT LEG INSIDE, including

all unlabeled tabs and gray areas.

G Glue RIGHT LEG INSIDE to HEAD at gray area 51.

H Detach LEFT LEG OUTSIDE and LEFT LEG EDGE A templates. Glue tabs 52–56 on LEFT LEG EDGE A to gray areas 52–56 on LEFT LEG OUTSIDE, including all unlabeled tabs and gray areas.

I Detach LEFT LEG EDGE B template. Glue tab 57 on LEFT LEG EDGE A to gray area 57 on LEFT LEG EDGE B. Glue tabs 58–63 on LEFT LEG EDGE B to gray areas 58–63 on left leg piece, including all unlabeled tabs and gray areas.

J Detach LEFT LEG EDGE C template. Glue tab 64 on LEFT LEG EDGE B to gray area 64 on LEFT LEG EDGE C. Glue tabs 65–70 on LEFT LEG EDGE C to gray areas on left leg piece, including all unlabeled tabs and gray areas.

K Detach LEFT LEG INSIDE template. Glue tabs 71–86 on left leg piece to gray areas 71–86 on LEFT LEG INSIDE, including all unlabeled tabs and gray areas.

L Glue LEFT LEG INSIDE to HEAD at gray area 87.

Rockmon lives among the rocks and stones of Red Rock Canyon, just outside of Las Vegas. Camouflaged to look like a pebble, Rockmon is only an inch tall. Although he's almost 100 years old, he's still considered a baby among rock monsters, whose life cycles span eons. Before Rockmon is fully grown, he will choose between remaining above ground and become a mountain, or traveling deep beneath the earth. Rock monsters who choose this second path are often—and correctly—blamed for earthquakes. Female rock monsters become volcanoes, and when they explode, lava spews and sputters out, which is how baby rock monsters are born.

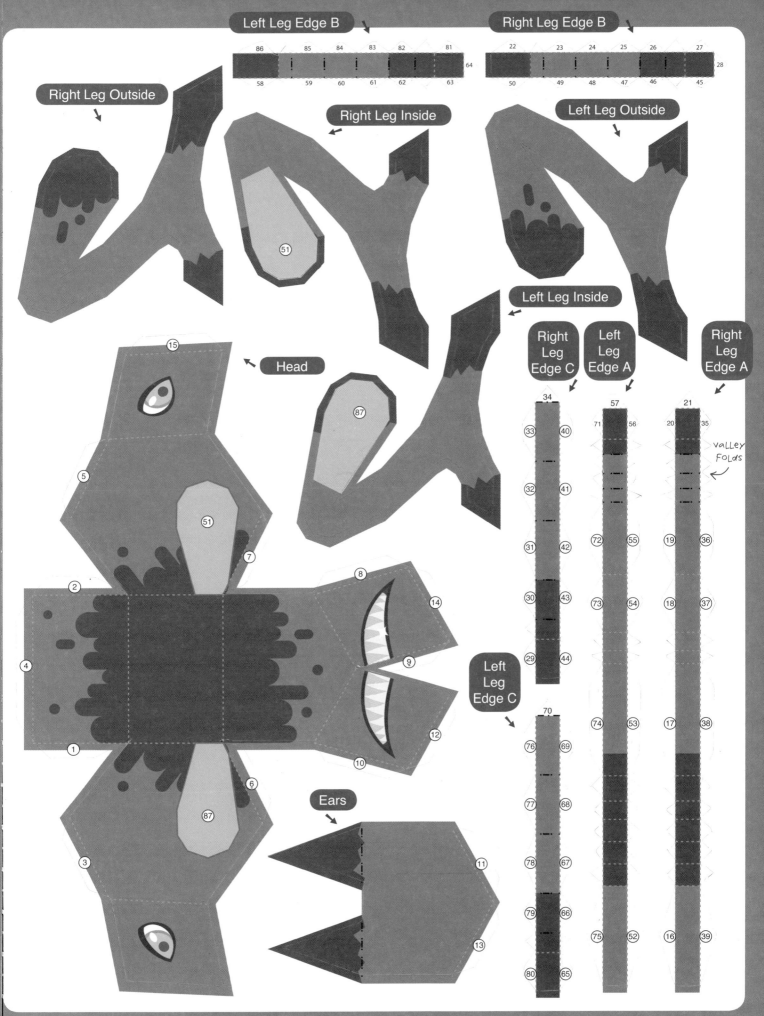

Left Leg Edge B

Right Leg Edge B

Right Leg Outside

Right Leg Inside

Left Leg Outside

Left Leg Inside

Right Leg Edge C

Left Leg Edge A

Right Leg Edge A

Head

valley folds

Left Leg Edge C

Ears

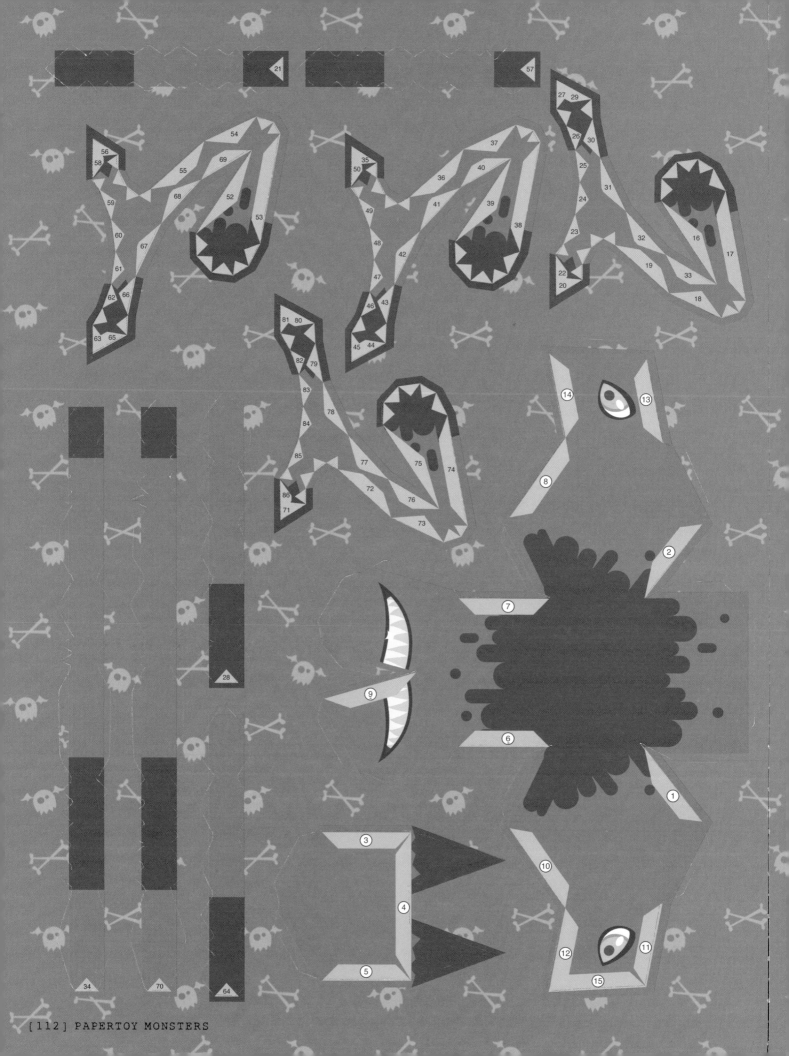

Wingy Wingy

TYPE: *Monstrum terrestrialis wingiwingi*

VARIANT NAMES: The Sweet Monster; Sweetie Pie

ORIGIN: cave in a village in Southeast Asia

DESCRIPTION: 4 feet tall; red skin; blonde hair; ear wings

ABILITIES: can fly; has night vision; can sing any pop song ever recorded

Discovered by Salazad

ASSEMBLY INSTRUCTIONS

A Detach HEAD and LEFT WING templates. Insert tabs 1–2 on LEFT WING into slots on left side of HEAD and glue to gray areas 1–2.

B Detach RIGHT WING template. Insert tabs 3–4 into slots on right side of HEAD and glue to gray areas 3–4.

C Glue tabs 5–15 on HEAD to gray areas 5–15.

D Detach BODY and RIGHT ARM templates. Insert tab 16 on RIGHT ARM into slot on right side of BODY and glue to gray area 16.

E Detach LEFT ARM template. Insert tab 17 into slot on left side of BODY and glue to gray area 17 on BODY.

F Remember to valley fold at legs on BODY so that they stick out. Glue tabs 18–24 on BODY to gray areas 18–24.

G Detach RIGHT HORN template. Glue tabs 25–27 to gray areas 25–27.

H Glue RIGHT HORN to HEAD at gray area 28.

I Detach LEFT HORN template. Glue tabs 29–31 to gray areas 29–31.

J Glue LEFT HORN to HEAD at gray area 32.

K Glue HEAD to BODY at gray area 33.

Wingy Wingy is a happy-go-lucky little winged monster from a cave somewhere in Southeast Asia whose main goal in life is to inspire people to love. With her superb night vision, Wingy enjoys wandering around the backyards of the houses in her village at night, when the world is most peaceful, chasing fireflies and blowing bubbles up to the stars while snacking on strawberry ice with rainbow sprinkles. The young human girls in her village enjoy spending time with Wingy Wingy because she will sit on their shoulders and whisper sweet stories in their ears, sing them songs, and laugh at their jokes. On occasion, she flies up to the treetops and brings down gifts for her friends: pinecones, beautiful leaves, and little vine-covered sticks. Wingy Wingy loves all creatures, except for the slow loris, whose eyes give her the creeps.

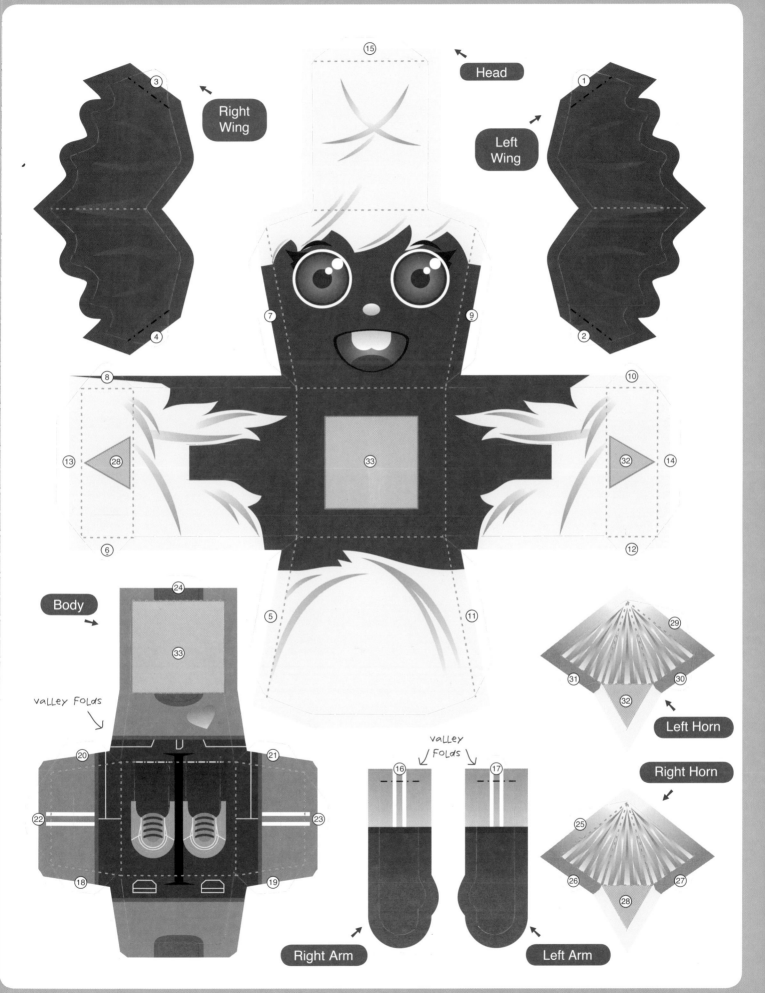

Right Wing

Head

Left Wing

Body

valley folds

Left Horn

Right Horn

valley folds

Right Arm

Left Arm

NOM NOM

TYPE: *Monstrum terrestrialis ratatouillius*

VARIANT NAME: The Mutant Rat Monster

ORIGIN: toxic waste dump, Detroit, Michigan, U.S.A.

DESCRIPTION: 150 feet tall; two large horns; green fur

ABILITIES: can chew through anything; excels at modern and interpretive dance

NOM NOM

Discovered by Jonny Chiba

ASSEMBLY INSTRUCTIONS

A Detach MONSTER BACK template. Glue tabs 1–2 to gray areas 1–2.

B Detach MONSTER FRONT template. Glue tabs 3–5 on MONSTER BACK to gray areas 3–5 on MONSTER FRONT.

C Detach CITY BLOCK template. Glue tabs 6–9 to gray areas 6–9.

D Detach CITY BACKGROUND template. Glue to CITY BLOCK at gray area 10.

E Insert tabs 11–12 on MONSTER BACK into slots on top of CITY BLOCK.

Nom Nom began his life as a common street rat, but everything changed after he stepped into a vat of green hazardous waste material in an undisclosed section of Detroit. Now Nom Nom is 150 feet tall and weighs somewhere in the neighborhood of 30 tons. Ravenous all the time, Nom Nom can consume an entire city block in less than 10 minutes: buildings, houses, cars (especially garbage trucks), and sidewalks. The more he eats, the bigger he gets—and the bigger he gets, the more he eats. Once he has gotten his teeth into a neighborhood, there is almost nothing that can stop him, and all he leaves behind is a cloud of dust.

ZOMBUNNY

TYPE: Monstrum extraterrestrialis zombunnicus

VARIANT NAMES: The Zombie Bunny Monster; Bugs Zombie

ORIGIN: secret government lab in Area 51

DESCRIPTION: 2 feet tall; bloody, gray decayed fur

ABILITIES: can eat 64 whole heads of lettuce in one bite

Discovered by Josh McKible

ASSEMBLY INSTRUCTIONS

A Detach BODY template. Glue tabs 1–7 to gray areas 1–7.

B Detach RIGHT LEG template. Glue tabs 8–13 to gray areas 8–13.

C Detach LEFT LEG template. Glue tabs 14–19 to gray areas 14–19.

D Detach TAIL template. Glue tabs 20–24 to gray areas 20–24.

E Detach RIGHT ARM template. Glue to BODY at gray area 25.

F Detach LEFT ARM template. Glue to BODY at gray area 26.

G Glue TAIL to BODY at gray area 27.

H Glue RIGHT LEG to BODY at gray area 28.

I Glue LEFT LEG to BODY at gray area 29.

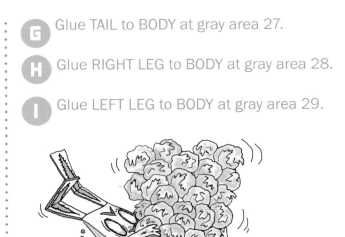

Zombunny is the product of a top-secret government experiment in life extension that went horribly wrong. Slow moving and easily confused, Zombunny roams the land in search of heads—heads of moldy lettuce, that is. He has been spotted in farmers' fields, backyard gardens, trash heaps, and the parking lots of supermarkets, where he sniffs the ground at night for remnants of forgotten vegetables. Known to decimate an entire supermarket produce section in less than 20 minutes, Zombunny is not considered harmful to humans unless they are wearing fur coats. And if you are wearing a rabbit fur, beware: He will go ballistic on you.

MUTANT, FOOD & THING MONSTERS

TYPE: *Monstrum mutantis lunchboxitus*

VARIANT NAMES: The Lunchbox Monster; Up-Chuck

ORIGIN: Flushing, Queens, U.S.A.

DESCRIPTION: 1 foot wide; covered with green slime

ABILITIES: can turn any food into a toxic substance; loses friends and alienates people

YUCKY CHUCK

TOXIC

YUCKY CHUCK

Discovered by Ben the Illustrator

ASSEMBLY INSTRUCTIONS

A Detach BODY template. Glue tabs 1–6 to gray areas 1–6.

B Detach LEFT LEG template. Glue tabs 7–13 to gray areas 7–13.

C Detach RIGHT LEG template. Glue tabs 14–20 to gray areas 14–20.

D Glue LEFT LEG to BODY at gray area 21.

E Glue RIGHT LEG to BODY at gray area 22.

F Detach HANDLE template. Insert tabs 23–24 into slots on top of BODY.

G Detach TOXIC TREATS templates. Glue or place in mouth.

Yucky Chuck is a mutant lunchbox monster who became toxic after sitting, forgotten, at the bottom of a child's locker during the summer of 1972. Once a happy lunchbox full of healthy treats, Chuck went nuclear when the tuna fish sandwich left inside him leeched a radioactive form of mercury into his innards. Not only did it make him rotten to the core, but now everything placed inside him becomes instantly toxic. The moment they come into contact with Chuck, sandwiches fester, juiceboxes reek, and eggs explode. The disgusting smell he emits is meant to make people upchuck. Yuck, Chuck.

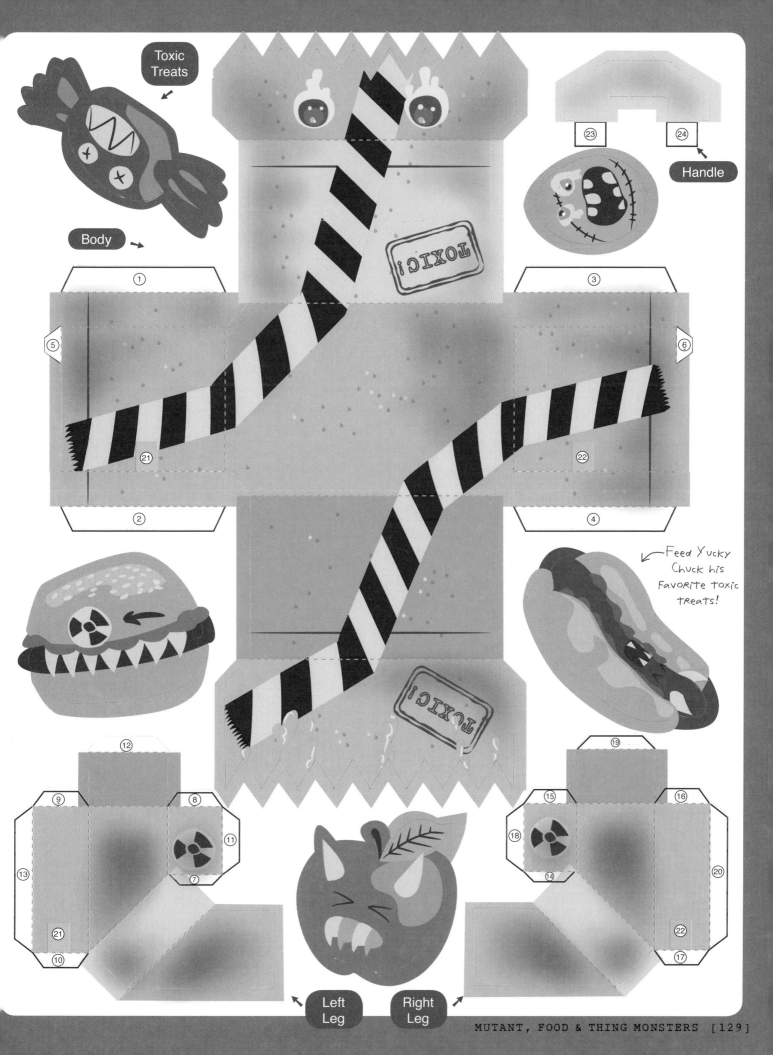

Toxic Treats

Body →

① ③ ⑤ ⑥ ② ④ �21 �22

¡TOXIC!

23 24

Handle

Feed Yucky Chuck his favorite toxic treats!

⑫ ⑲
⑨ ⑧ ⑮ ⑯
⑪ ⑱
⑦ ⑭
⑬ ⑳
�21 �221
⑩ ⑰

Left Leg   Right Leg

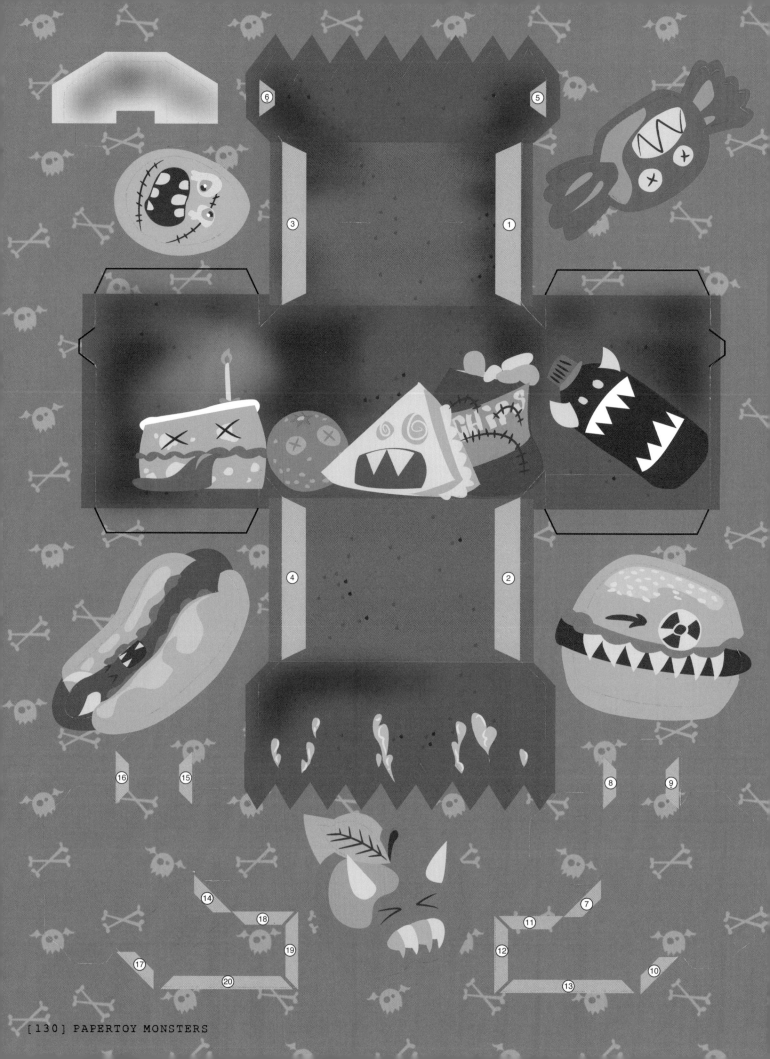

THE BLOB

TYPE: *Monstrum mutantis sluma*
VARIANT NAMES: The Trash Blob; The Goo
ORIGIN: New York City, U.S.A.
DESCRIPTION: 400 feet tall, gooey, jellylike, stinky
ABILITIES: lifting garbage trucks, frightening small
children, beatboxing

THE BLOB

Discovered by Dolly Oblong

ASSEMBLY INSTRUCTIONS

A Detach FRONT and TONGUE templates. Glue tab 1 on TONGUE to gray area 1 on FRONT so it sticks out of the mouth.

B Detach CENTER template. Curve, then glue tabs 2–23 to gray areas 2–23 on FRONT, including all unlabeled tabs and gray areas.

C Detach BACK template. Glue tabs 24–45 on CENTER to gray areas 24–45 on BACK, including all unlabeled tabs and gray areas.

D Detach LEFT ARM template. Insert tab 46 into slot on left side of CENTER.

E Detach RIGHT ARM template. Insert tab 47 into slot on right side of CENTER.

The Blob began its life as a hamster-size ball of slime in the sewers of New York City. The original slime was a mixture of discarded wads of gum and the gunk found inside sewage pipes, but as other garbage started sticking to it, The Blob grew to enormous proportions. He continues to live and roam in the sewers of Manhattan, but on warm nights he slimes his way to garbage dumps or junkyards and feeds on crunchy car fenders and discarded baby strollers. The Blob doesn't like it when the temperature drops below freezing, as it makes his gooey substance very stiff. He is naturally friendly but wary of humans, who tend to run screaming at the mere sight of him.

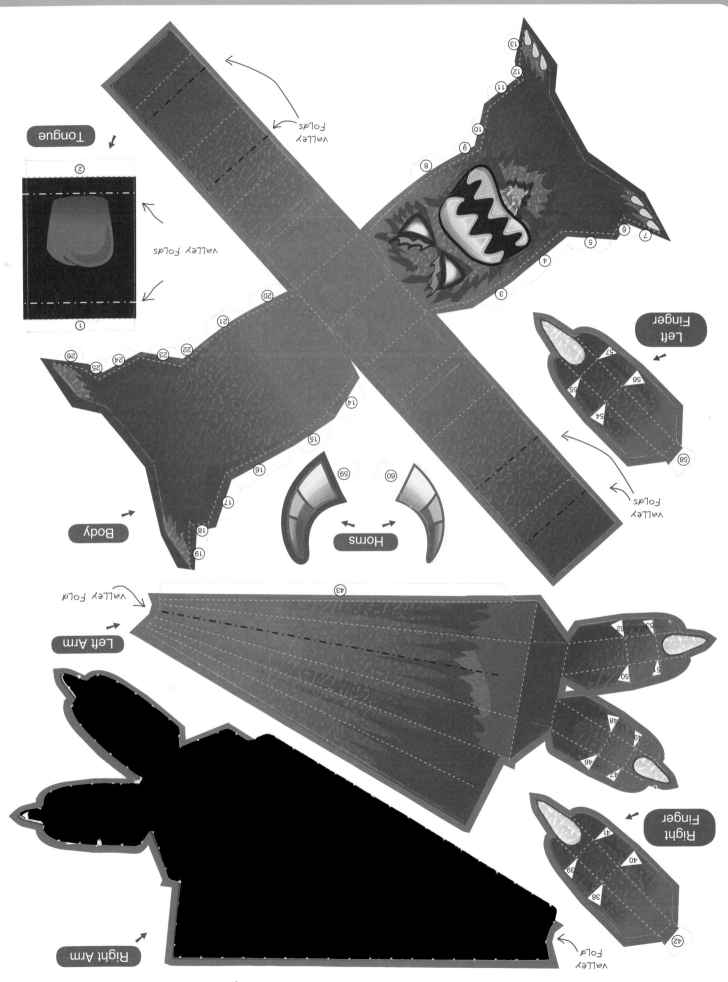

Tongue

Valley Folds

Valley Folds

Left Finger

Valley Folds

Body

Horns

Left Arm

Valley Fold

Right Finger

Right Arm

Valley Fold

GRIMP

TYPE: *Monstrum mutantis seamonkeetus*

VARIANT NAME: The Sea Monkey Mutant Monster

ORIGIN: bedroom, Utah, U.S.A.

DESCRIPTION: looks like a pile of toys with eyes

ABILITIES: can build the most complex Lego projects in seconds; has perfect aim

GRIMP

Discovered by 3EyedBear

ASSEMBLY INSTRUCTIONS

A Detach BODY template. Glue together at gray areas 1–4.

B Detach BASE template. Glue BASE to BODY at gray areas 5–6.

Grimp was born under a pile of clothes and toys that had been accumulating over a ten-month span in the bedroom of a boy named Butch Greeser. Butch's room had become so messy during that period that he kept losing things in the filth: bits of toys, dirty underwear, slices of pizza, empty milk containers, et cetera. When a Sea Monkey kit accidentally broke on the floor in Butch's room, the sea monkey larva merged with a group of maggots living on an old Subway sandwich at the bottom of Butch's trash heap. The resulting mutant life-form then began to swallow the toys that surrounded it, which added to its genetic makeup and girth—eventually becoming the monstrosity known as Grimp. No longer living in Greeser's room, Grimp now roams Utah's highways in his toy car, flinging trash at passing vehicles.

VALLEY FOLD

Body

Base

HEIDI

TYPE: *Monstrum mutantis inclosetum*

VARIANT NAME: The Monster in Your Closet

ORIGIN: Bavaria, Germany

DESCRIPTION: 7 feet tall, jagged teeth, polka-dotted

ABILITIES: can vanish into thin air as if by magic, yodeling

HEIDI

Discovered by Marshall Alexander

ASSEMBLY INSTRUCTIONS

A Detach BODY template. Glue tabs 1–14 to gray areas 1–14.

B Detach DOOR template. Glue tabs 15–16 on BODY to gray areas 15–16 on DOOR.

Heidi is an oversized bug monster that lives inside closets. She began her life as a dust mite in the sneaker of Helga, a young girl in Bavaria, mutating into her present state after Helga began feeding her vast quantities of fish food and Wiener schnitzel. Eventually, Heidi grew to be as large as the door frame and hardly ever ventured outside the closet. But after Helga grew up and moved away, Heidi had no choice but to get out on her own to forage for food. She now roams the suburbs of Germany, breaking into people's houses to find shelter in their closets. On occasion, and without meaning to, Heidi scares young children who catch a glimpse of her. By the time the children have called for their parents, Heidi has vanished as if by magic, and the kids are stuck trying to convince the grown-ups they really did see a monster in their closet.

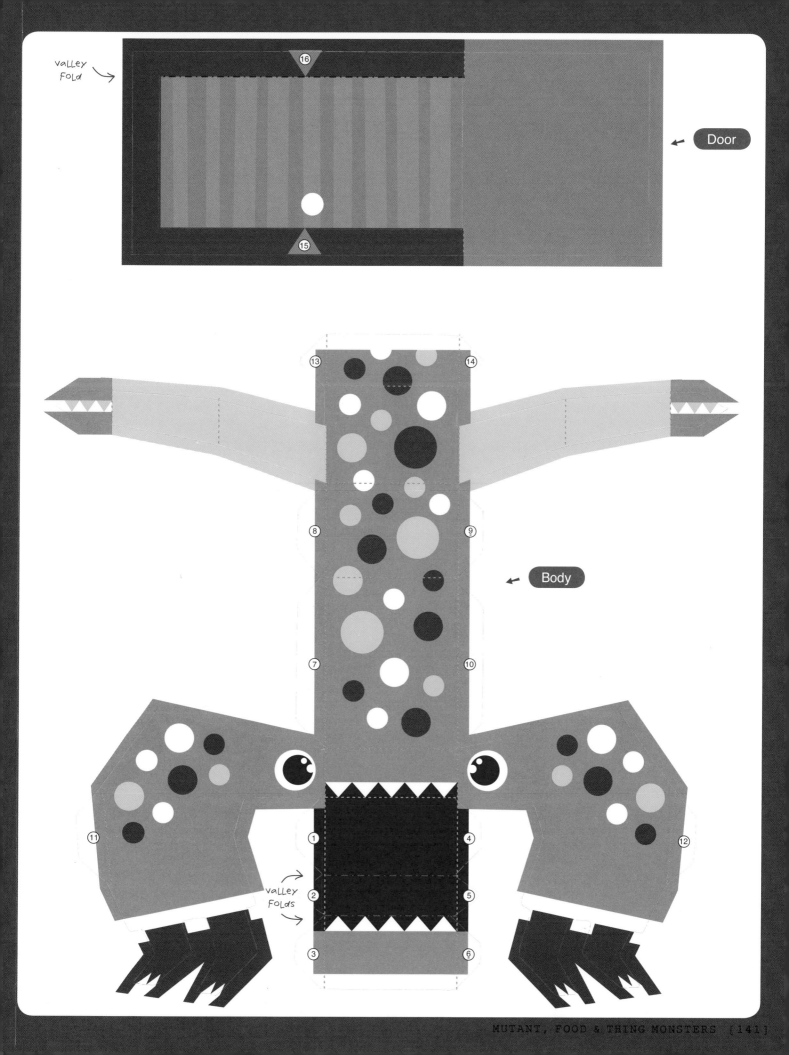

VALLEY FOLD →

Door ←

⑯
⑮

⑬ ⑭

⑧ ⑨

Body ←

⑦ ⑩

⑪ ⑫

① ④

VALLEY FOLDS

② ⑤

③ ⑥

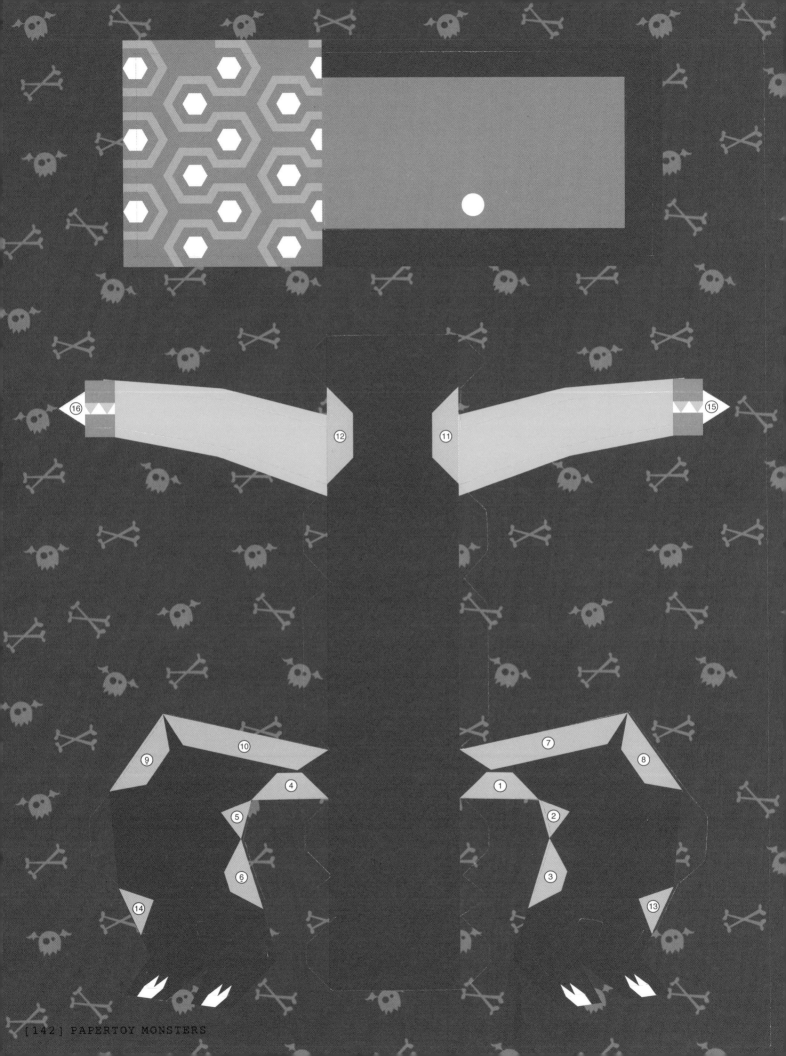

ZEKE

TYPE:	*Monstrum mutantis underbeddus*
VARIANT NAME:	The Monster Under Your Bed
ORIGIN:	Bavaria, Germany
DESCRIPTION:	4-feet wide; six legs; large eyes
ABILITIES:	has catlike stealth; can speak 62½ different languages

Discovered by Marshall Alexander

ASSEMBLY INSTRUCTIONS

A Detach BODY template. Glue tabs 1–10 to gray areas 1–10.

B Detach BED and HEADBOARD templates. Glue tabs 11–13 on BED to gray areas 11–13 on HEADBOARD.

C Detach FOOTBOARD template. Glue tabs 14–16 on BED to gray areas 14–16 on FOOTBOARD.

D Glue BODY to BED at gray area 17.

Zeke began his life as a bedbug in the same room as Heidi, the monster in the closet, and he grew to his enormous proportions for the same reason: Helga overfed him. It wasn't fish food and Wiener schnitzels that Zeke ate, though, but a steady diet of donut holes, liverwurst, and fried onion rings. As a result, Zeke reeks. A few months after Helga moved away, Zeke was forced to abandon his home under her bed and seek shelter elsewhere. He tried various situations, traveling far and wide, and eventually found a place to live under a bed in a youth hostel in Bergen. Zeke is remarkably social, thanks to his friendship with Helga. However, because of his size, he can't help but frighten people when he comes out from under the bed—especially when this happens in the middle of the night. Between his talent for scaring people and the foul smell he emits, Zeke tries to stay under the bed as much as possible.

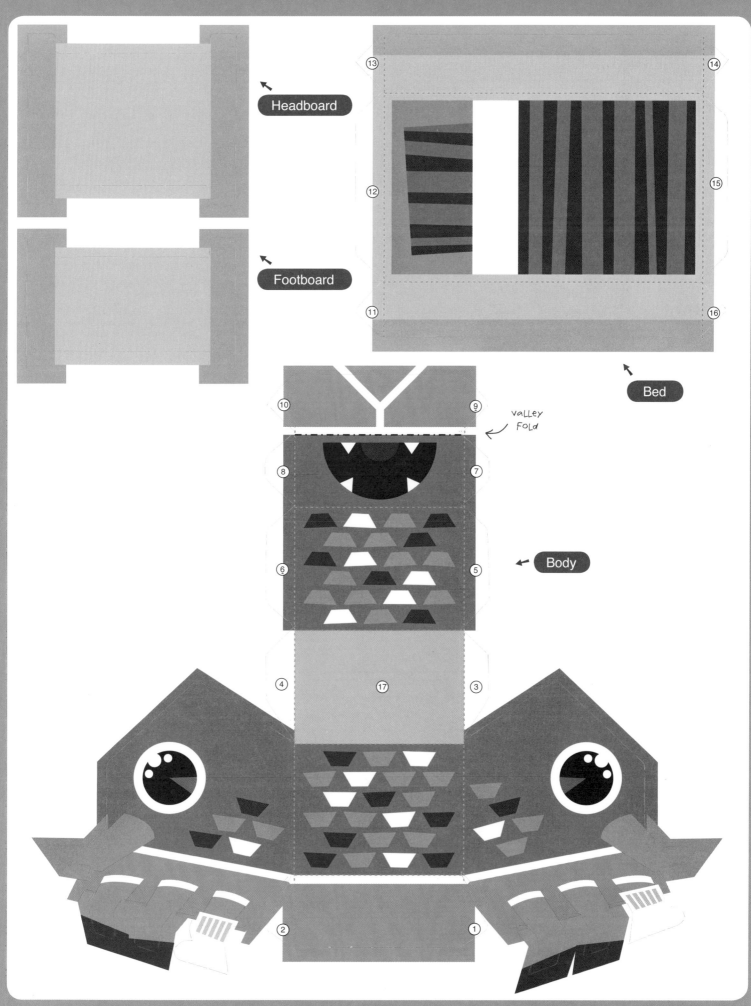

Headboard

Footboard

Bed

VALLEY FOLD

Body

TYPE: *Monstrum mutantis zoomzoomicus*
VARIANT NAME: The Fender Bender Monster
ORIGIN: Detroit, Michigan, U.S.A.
DESCRIPTION: 11 feet tall, three eyes, horned (Cab);
2 feet tall, one eye (Lyle)
ABILITIES: 0-60 in .5 seconds

CAB & LYLE

Discovered by Matt Hawkins

ASSEMBLY INSTRUCTIONS

 A Detach CAB template. Curve head and glue tabs 1–10 to gray areas 1–10.

 B Detach RIGHT FOOT template. Glue tab 11 to gray area 11.

C Detach LEFT FOOT template. Glue tab 12 to gray area 12.

 D Insert tabs 13–14 on RIGHT FOOT into slots on bottom of BODY and glue to gray areas 13–14.

 E Insert tabs 15–16 on LEFT FOOT into slots on bottom of BODY and glue to gray areas 15–16.

 F Detach RIGHT ARM template. Insert tab 17 into slot on right side of BODY and glue to gray area 17.

 G Detach LEFT ARM template. Insert tab 18 into slot on left side of BODY and glue to gray area 18.

H Detach RIGHT HORN template. Insert tab 19 into slot on right side of BODY.

I Detach LEFT HORN template. Insert tab 20 into slot on left side of BODY.

J Detach LYLE template. Glue tabs 21–24 to gray areas 21–24.

K Detach LYLE'S HAT template. Insert tab 25 into slot on top of LYLE.

L Detach LYLE'S TENTACLE template. Insert tab 26 into slot on side of LYLE.

M Detach NOSE template. Insert tab 27 into slot on front of BODY.

N Place LYLE in mouth of CAB.

 Cab and Lyle are always together. They first met as young monsterlings in Detroit, where they lived with their parents inside an auto parts factory. Cab, the larger of the two, drinks diesel fuel and motors around like a mad monster. He doesn't obey traffic laws and does not meet any environmental standards. Lyle, the smaller one, is more responsible, getting regular tune-ups and adhering to a strict diet of organic biodiesel fuel. Years ago, he soldered a steering wheel into Cab's mouth so that he could drive him around. Cab and Lyle can usually be found hanging around parking lots so they can sneak up behind people carrying shopping bags full of groceries, scaring them senseless and causing innumerable fender benders.

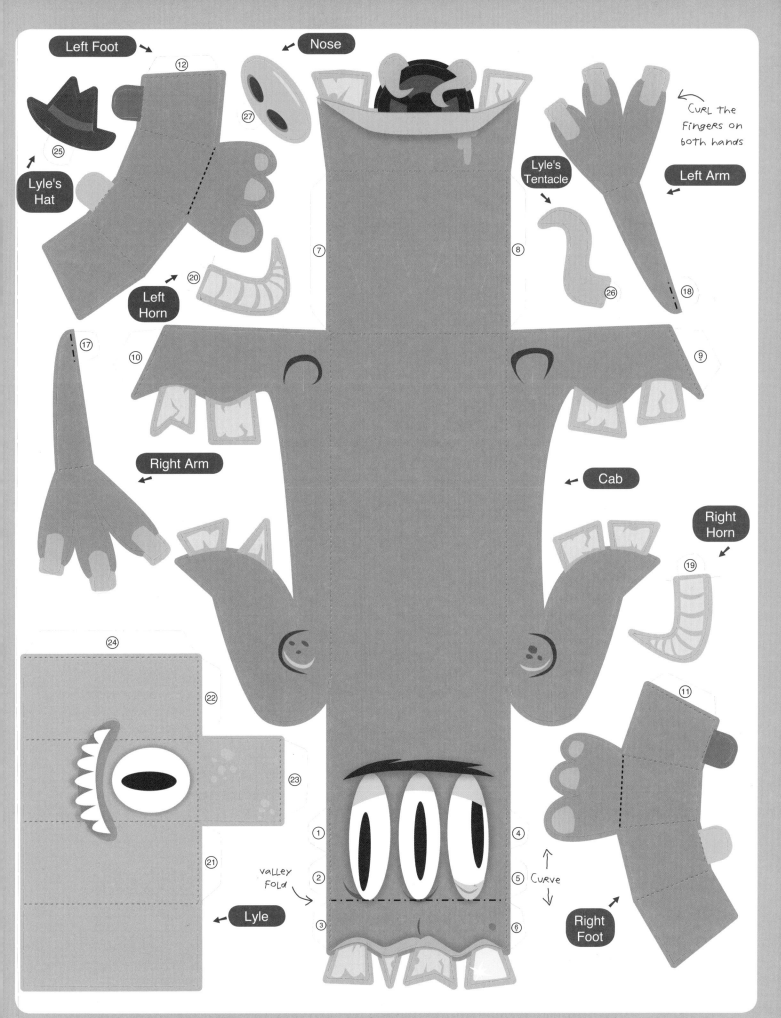

Left Foot

Nose

⑫

㉗

Curl the fingers on both hands

Left Arm

㉕

Lyle's Hat

Lyle's Tentacle

⑦

⑧

⑳

Left Horn

㉖

⑱

⑰

⑩

⑨

Right Arm

Cab

Right Horn

⑲

㉔

⑪

㉒

㉓

① ④

⑤ Curve

㉑

② Valley Fold

Right Foot

Lyle

③ ⑥

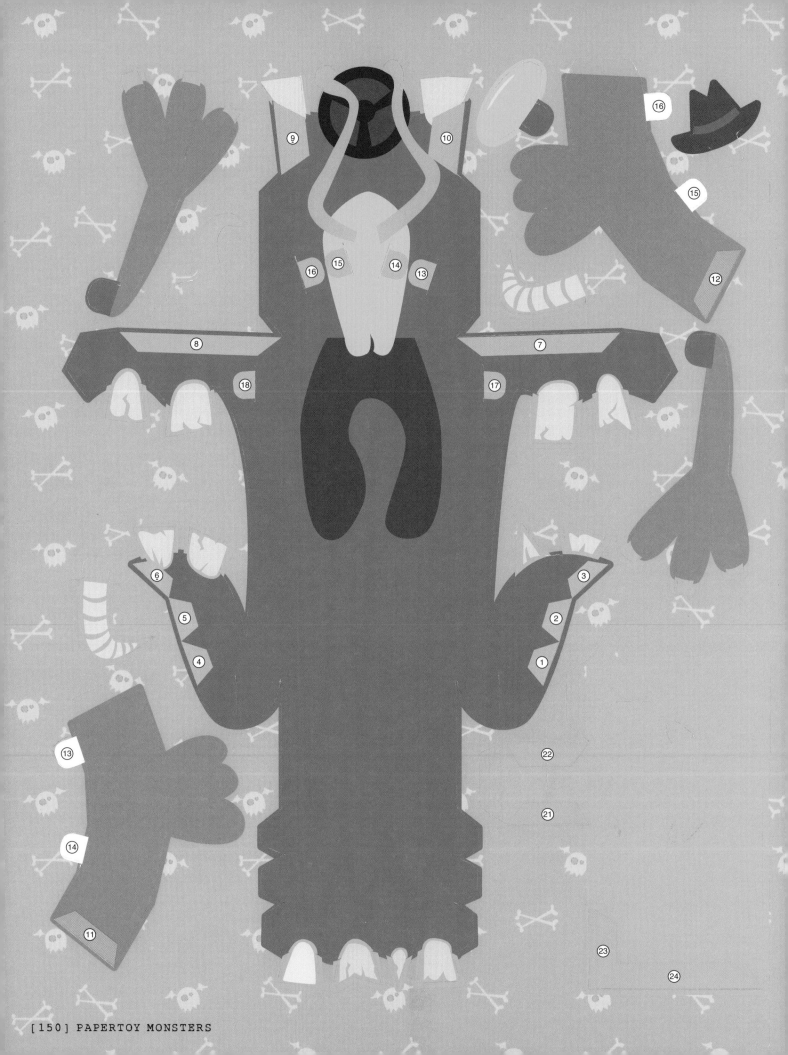

Philo

TYPE: *Monstrum mutantis electricus*
VARIANT NAMES: The TV Monster; Dream Snatcher
ORIGIN: Devils Lake, North Dakota, U.S.A.
DESCRIPTION: 20-inch-wide screen; wormlike arms
ABILITIES: sucking humans' dreams out of them; turning them into couch potatoes; procrastination

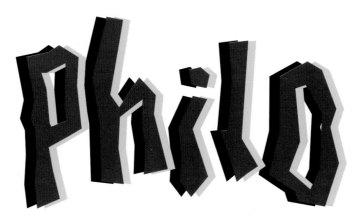

Discovered by Scott Schaller

ASSEMBLY INSTRUCTIONS

A Detach MOUTH template. Glue tabs 1–4 to gray areas 1–4.

B Detach BODY template. Glue tabs 5–8 on MOUTH to gray areas 5–8 on BODY.

C Glue tabs 9–12 on BODY to gray areas 9–12.

D Detach TENTACLE A–D templates. Glue tabs 13–16 to gray areas 13–16 on inside of MOUTH.

E Detach ANTENNA. Insert tab 17 into slot on top of BODY.

Philo is a TV monster, said to be the ghost of a couch potato whose angry soul became trapped inside an old wooden TV set. Inhabiting a world of electricity and cathode tubes, Philo watches people as they watch him. Then, when his viewers have fallen asleep, his tentacles creep out of the TV cabinet and close in on his victims. He sucks the dreams right out of them for his own entertainment, preferring their far more original content to the choices available on his own outdated basic-channels-only set. Philo has a special fondness for nightmares involving unprepared test-takers and falling.

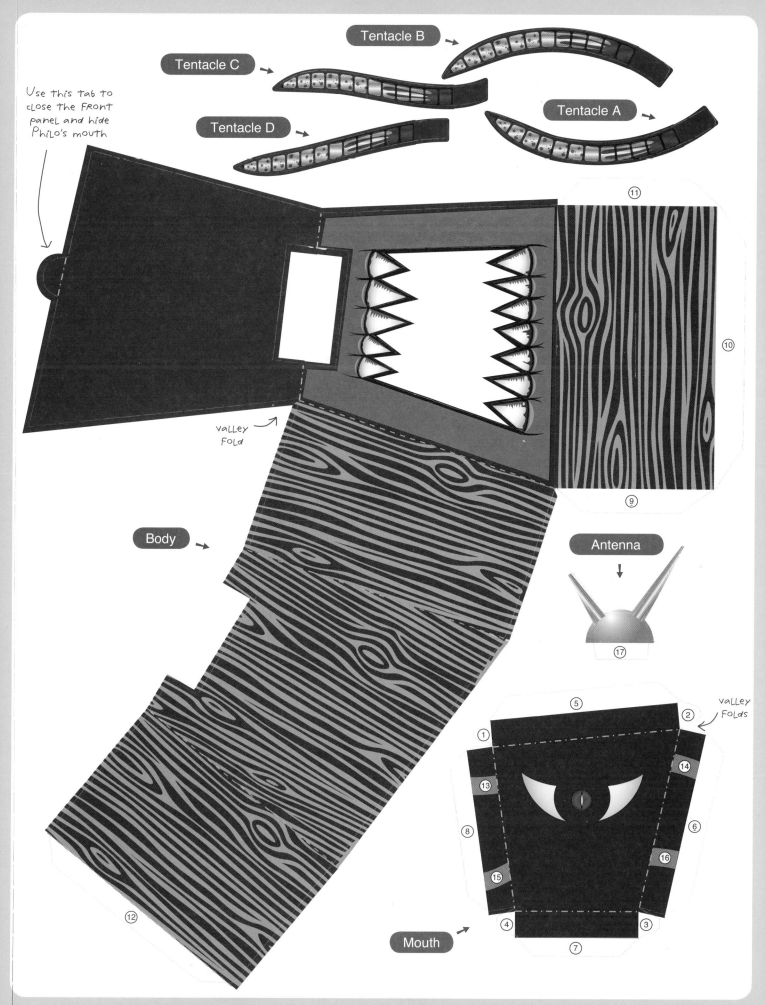

Tentacle B

Tentacle C

Tentacle D

Tentacle A

Use this tab to close the FRONT panel and hide Philo's mouth

11

10

9

VALLEY FOLD

Body

Antenna

17

VALLEY FOLDS

5

2

1

14

13

8

6

16

15

4

3

12

Mouth

7

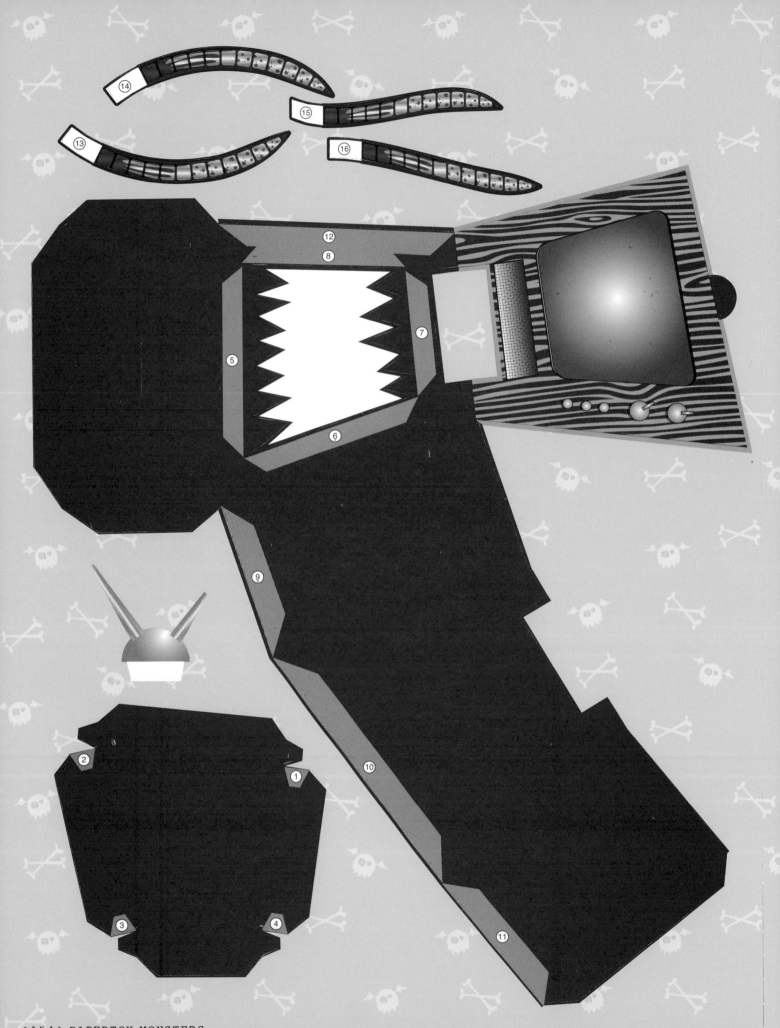

Halloweeny

TYPE: *Monstrum mutanis trickortreatus*

VARIANT NAME: The Halloween Monster

ORIGIN: unknown

DESCRIPTION: 4 feet tall; mask that covers his head

ABILITIES: can convince anyone to give him candy; teeth are resistant to cavities

Halloweeny

Discovered by Rememberthelittleguy

ASSEMBLY INSTRUCTIONS

A Detach BODY template. Glue tabs 1–4 to gray areas 1–4.

B Detach RIGHT ARM and LEFT ARM templates. Glue tab 5 on RIGHT ARM to gray area 5 on BODY. Glue tab 6 on LEFT ARM to gray area 6 on BODY.

C Detach MASK template. Glue tabs 7–10 to gray areas 7–10. Place MASK on top of BODY.

What makes Halloween so spooky is that you never really know what lurks beneath everyone else's costumes. You might see a couple of kids dressed up as Darth Vader and Chewbacca and assume they're average eight-year-old kids. Little would you suspect that there might be a real monster hidden underneath. Pull the mask off that girl wearing a Princess Fiona costume—you may actually find a real ogre! The thing is, you never know, which is why Halloweeny loves Halloween so much. As a genuine monster, he gets to trick-or-treat and pretend he's just like every other kid on the block. The rest of the year, Halloweeny lives in an old abandoned house, refining his creepy image and practicing his mandolin.

EVIL ICY

TYPE: *Monstrum mutanitis refrigeratus*
VARIANT NAME: The Ice-Cream Monster
ORIGIN: Mister Softscoop Ice Cream truck refrigerator
DESCRIPTION: 6 inches tall; cone-shaped head; oozey
ABILITIES: can turn most objects into goo; has an evil
laugh that will make you shiver with fear (and cold)

EVIL ICY

Discovered by Nick Knite

ASSEMBLY INSTRUCTIONS

A Detach ICE CREAM template. Glue tabs 1–8 to gray areas 1–8.

B Detach CONE template. Glue tab 9 to gray area 9.

C Place CONE on top of ICE CREAM.

Evil Icy is an angry little scoop of mutant ice cream. It is believed that this formerly tasty treat mutated into a twisted monster after a dispute between a wizard and a mad scientist turned ugly. Both parties claimed an abandoned building—conveniently and deliciously located next door to a Mister Softscoop Ice Cream truck parking lot—as their new evil headquarters. When neither would back down, a showdown between magic and science turned the contents of all the parked Mister Softscoop trucks into "I Scream" monsters. Fortunately a heat wave caused them to melt—except for Evil Icy, who had the good sense to wait inside the freezer until it passed. Evil Icy is best avoided if you wish to remain in a solid state—one slimy touch from the creature will turn you into a melted mess.

TYPE: *Monstrum mutantis toasticus*

VARIANT NAMES: The Bread Monster; Dread the Bread

ORIGIN: the streets, Los Angeles, California, U.S.A.

DESCRIPTION: 4 inches wide; long tongue

ABILITIES: tongue is a lethal weapon; excellent tongue-eye coordination

TONGUE TOASTIE

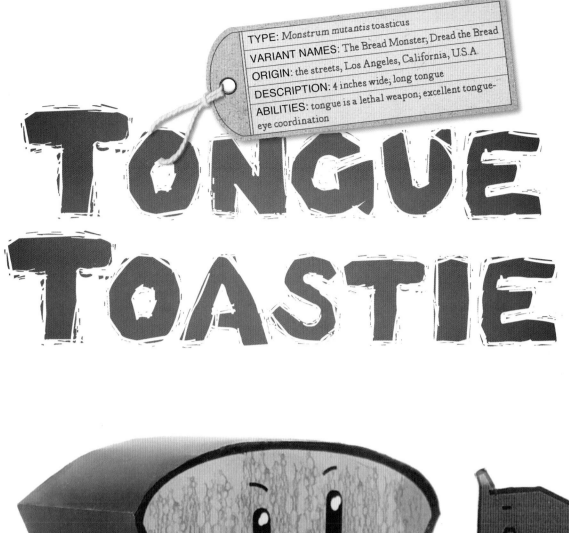

TONGUE TOASTIE

Discovered by Nick Knite

ASSEMBLY INSTRUCTIONS

A Detach TOAST template. Curve long section and glue tabs 1–31 to gray areas 1–31.

B Detach TONGUE template. Glue TONGUE to TOAST at gray area 32.

Tongue Toastie is one terrible slice of bread. Originally part of a pastrami, salami, ham, anchovies, pickles, and mayonnaise sandwich, Toastie turned bitter and resentful after being separated from the rest of his sandwich by the would-be eater. Tossed into the street like, well, yesterday's toast, Toastie spent a few nights on the tough streets of Los Angeles before a clumsy janitor dropped him into a water purification facility. In just two short weeks, this former tasty slice of toast had turned into an irate monster with an appetite for destruction. Though he has no arms, he has grown a mighty tongue that he uses with great skill. Toastie can lash out at his enemies or lick food off a plate several feet away. When he is not out destroying things and cleaning plates, Toastie enjoys lawn bowling.

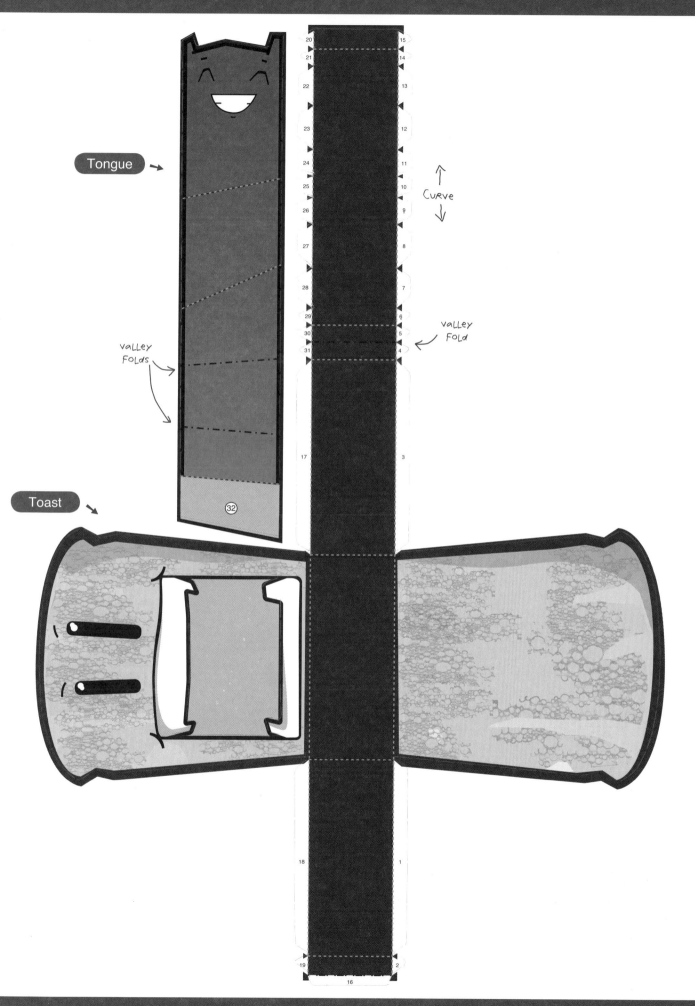

Tongue

Toast

valley
folds

valley
folds

Curve

valley
fold

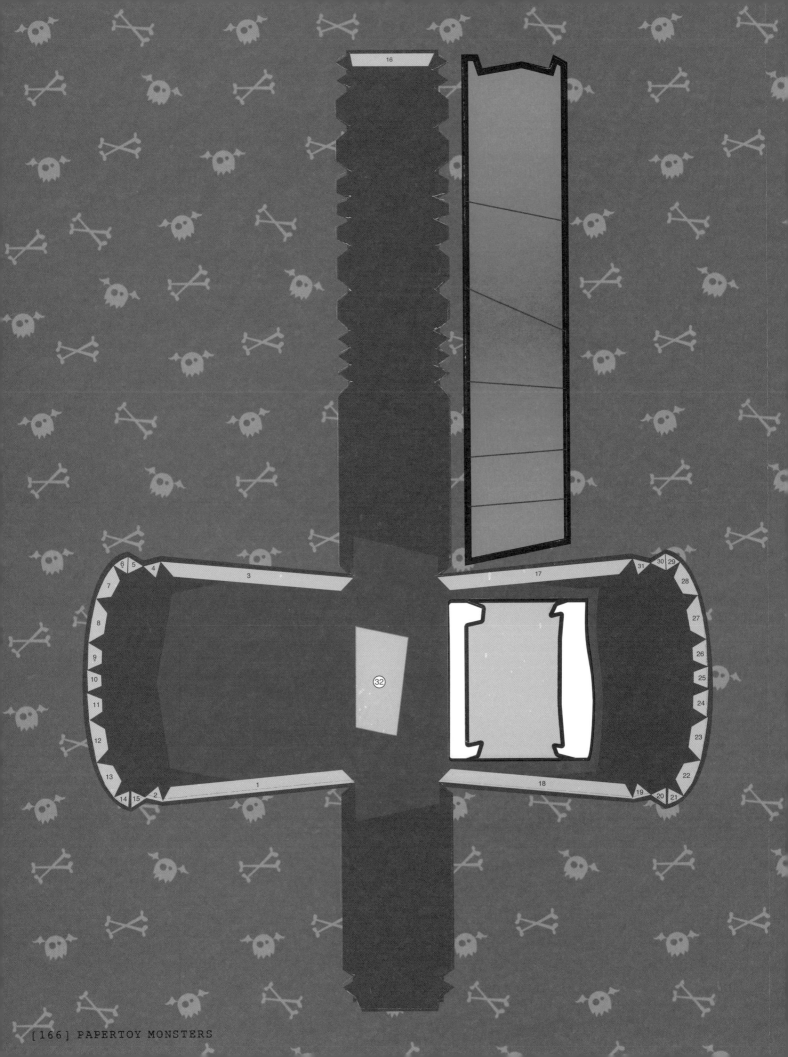

CUBETTO

TYPE: *Monstrum mutantis iciculis*
VARIANT NAMES: The Ice Monster; The Rude Cube
ORIGIN: the Alps, Italy
DESCRIPTION: 7 inches wide; rectangular; icy
ABILITIES: melts and refreezes at will; has a photographic memory

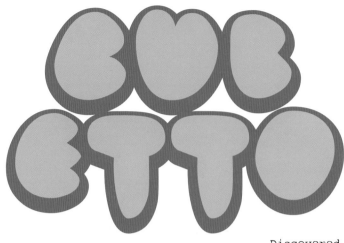

Discovered by Filippo Perin, aka PHIL

ASSEMBLY INSTRUCTIONS

A Detach BODY template. Glue tabs 1–4 to gray areas 1–4.

B Detach MOUTH template. Glue tabs 5–8 to gray areas 5–8.

C Detach EYES template. Glue tabs 9–12 to gray areas 9–12.

D Detach LEFT LEG template. Glue tab 13 to gray area 13.

E Detach RIGHT LEG template. Glue tab 14 to gray area 14.

F Detach LEFT FOOT template. Glue tabs 15–21 to gray areas 15–21.

G Detach RIGHT FOOT template. Glue tabs 22–28 to gray areas 22–28.

H Place MOUTH over BODY and glue tabs 29–32 on BODY to gray areas 29–32 on inside of MOUTH.

I Place EYES over MOUTH and glue tabs 33–36 on EYES to gray areas 33–36 on top of MOUTH.

J Insert bottom of RIGHT LEG into star-shaped slot on RIGHT FOOT.

K Insert bottom of LEFT LEG into star-shaped slot on LEFT FOOT.

L Insert top of RIGHT LEG into star-shaped slot on bottom right of BODY.

M Insert top of LEFT LEG into star-shaped slot on bottom left of BODY.

Cubetto was born in the depths of an abandoned freezer found inside a garbage truck that was caught under an avalanche in the Italian Alps. The truck, which disappeared en route to its destination some 35 years ago, was found only recently after global warming had thawed the bottom of the snow pack, allowing Cubetto to escape his icy grave. Thought to be the result of a toxic combination of battery acid and windshield wiper fluid, combined with the freezing temperatures and some unfortunately located radioactive ice, Cubetto has mutated into one despicable ice cube. Beware of this icy creature: With the ability to melt into water and refreeze at will, he can sneak up on you when you least expect it. Just one touch will turn you instantly into an oversize ice cube. Skiers most often fall victim to Cubetto, turning up frozen at the bottom of the ski slopes.

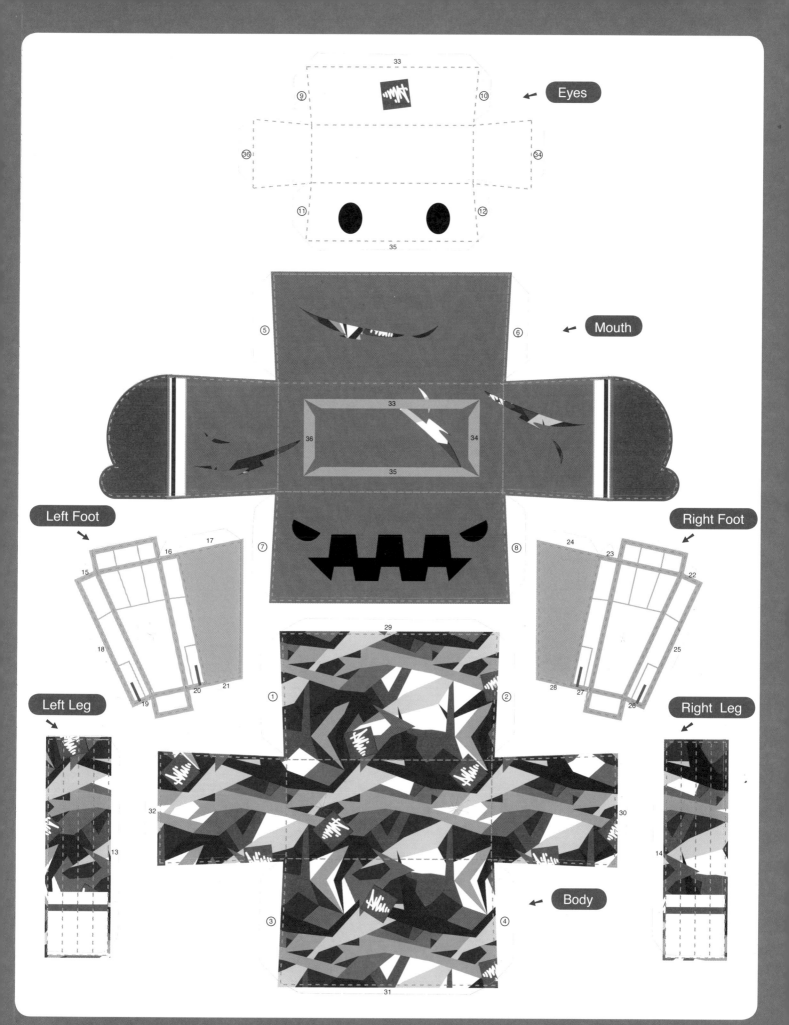

Eyes

Mouth

Left Foot

Right Foot

Left Leg

Right Leg

Body

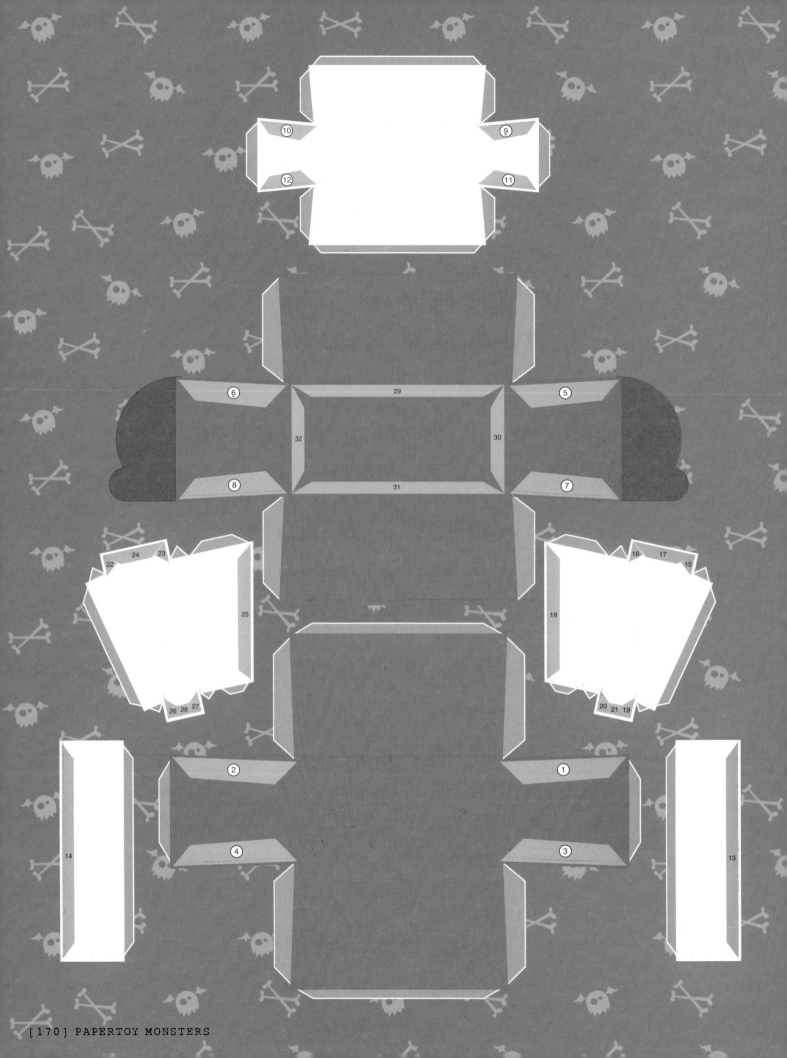

HUMAN MONSTERS

GRUMPY GRAMPS

TYPE: *Monstrum humanus grumpilicus*

VARIANT NAME: The Grampa Monster

ORIGIN: Tweed, Scotland

DESCRIPTION: short; stout; hairy

ABILITIES: knows the Latin terms for 321 types of mustaches; inventing insults to hurl at young whippersnappers

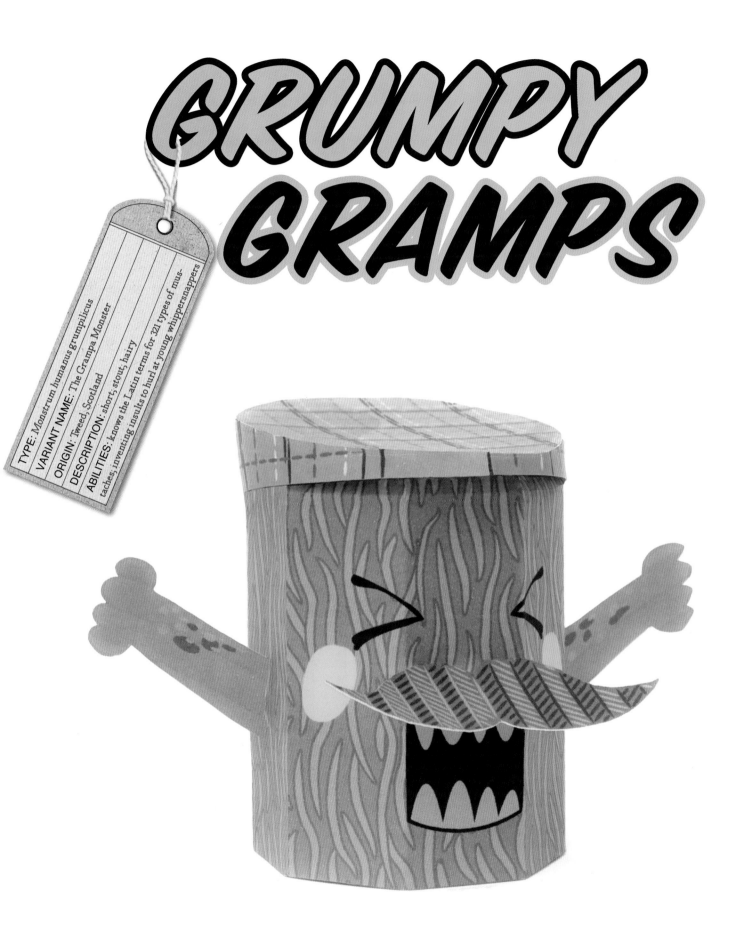

GRUMPY GRAMPS

Discovered by Ben the Illustrator

ASSEMBLY INSTRUCTIONS

A Detach HEAD template. Glue tabs 1–7 to gray areas 1–7.

B Detach LEFT ARM template. Insert tab 8 into slot on left side of HEAD.

C Detach RIGHT ARM template. Insert tab 9 into slot on right side of HEAD.

D Detach HAT template. Curve long section and glue tabs 10–25 to gray areas 10–25. Glue HAT to HEAD at gray area 26.

E Select and detach a MUSTACHE template and insert tabs into slots above mouth. You can change Grumpy Gramps's mustache whenever you want!

Grumpy Gramps is a 99-year-old monster from the village of Tweed in Scotland. Discovered living inside the musty suitcase of the town's only barber, Gramps has a collection of mustaches of various shapes and sizes. Every day he chooses the mustache that best matches one of his seven crotchety moods: bad-tempered, cantankerous, crabby, grouchy, grumbling, irritable, and peevish. No one knows why he's so surly. It may be because his diet consists solely of smelly cheese on cold, dry toast and flat soda. It may be because he hasn't showered in 50 years. Either way, Grumpy Gramps dislikes everything (except classical music) and everyone (except the town barber). The only thing that makes him laugh is when he draws fake-looking mustaches on people's pictures in magazines.

Lord Leonard

TYPE: *Monstrum humanus daemonicus*

VARIANT NAMES: The Goat Monster; Goat Boy

ORIGIN: France

DESCRIPTION: 12 feet tall; horns; wears a long cloak

ABILITIES: fine artist; can talk to the dead; knows 1,362 distinct bird calls

Lord Leonard

Discovered by Horrorwood

ASSEMBLY INSTRUCTIONS

A Detach BODY template. Glue tabs 1–6 to gray areas 1–6.

B Detach LEFT ARM template. Curve hand around a pen or pencil and glue tab 7 to gray area 7.

C Detach RIGHT ARM template. Curve hand around a pen or pencil and glue tab 8 to gray area 8.

D Glue LEFT ARM to BODY at gray area 9.

E Glue RIGHT ARM to BODY at gray area 10.

F Lord Leonard likes to hold a pencil as a staff. Place any pen or pencil through the holes his hands create.

Lord Leonard is a curious creature. Beginning his life as a goat, he was transformed into his current humanoid state at the age of ten by Lord Antoine of Gobigne, who is said to have been the first demon settler in the Languedoc region of France. Treated like a son, Leonard became sole heir to Gobigne's vast fortune and estate. He was educated at the Sorbonne in Paris, where he majored in beaux arts and minored in demonology, the latter chosen after he wished to exact revenge on his fellow students who would taunt him with malicious calls of "Goat Boy!" as he attempted to paint his next masterpiece. Now rude and generally unpleasant, Lord Leonard lives in a luxuriously decorated tower in his castle with his loyal servant, Lambert, a sheep he transformed into a human about a century ago. When he is not drawing or painting—he prefers lovely little landscapes—Lord Leonard can be found exercising his demonic paranormal abilities, communing with the dead, dropping rocks onto the heads of curious tourists looking to catch a glimpse of The Goat Monster, and bird-watching.

Left Arm

Body

Right Arm

Curve

Curve

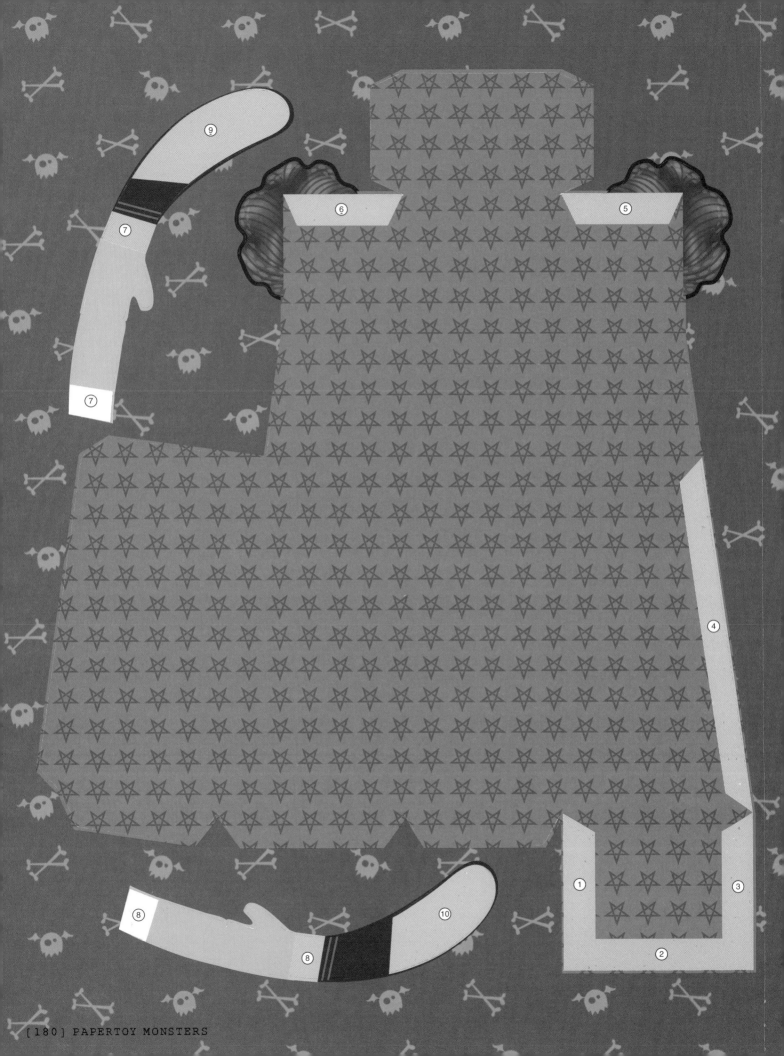

Lambert

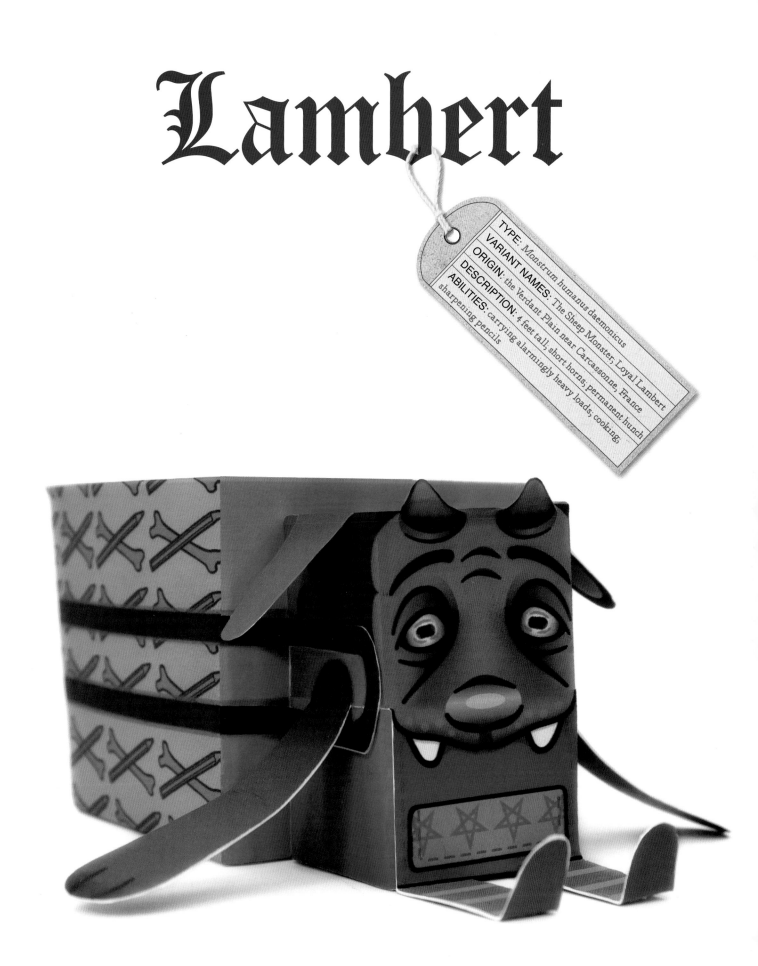

TYPE: *Monstrum humanus daemonicus*

VARIANT NAMES: The Sheep Monster; Loyal Lambert

ORIGIN: the Verdant Plain near Carcassonne, France

DESCRIPTION: 4 feet tall; short horns; permanent hunch

ABILITIES: carrying alarmingly heavy loads; cooking; sharpening pencils

Lambert

Discovered by Horrorwood

ASSEMBLY INSTRUCTIONS

1. Detach BODY template. Glue tabs 1–8 to gray areas 1–8.

2. Detach BOX template. Glue tabs 9–12 to gray areas 9–12.

3. Detach LEFT STRAP template. Glue to BODY at gray area 13.

4. Detach RIGHT STRAP template. Glue to BODY at gray area 14.

5. Glue BODY to BOX at gray area 15.

6. Glue tabs 16–17 on LEFT STRAP to gray areas 16–17 on BOX.

7. Glue tabs 18–19 on RIGHT STRAP to gray areas 18–19 on BOX.

We should convert to gas heat...

Lambert is a 100-year-old demon from the Verdant Plain, located deep within the Dark Realm near Carcassonne, France. Faithful servant to Lord Leonard, an artist with demonic powers, Lambert is grateful to his master for saving him from becoming every sheep's worst nightmare: mutton. Now instead of becoming dinner, Lambert serves it, acting as Leonard's personal chef. Additional duties include carrying heavy loads of wood on his back to stoke the gigantic hearth in Lord Leonard's castle, throwing an assortment of kitchen utensils at pesky human loiterers, and sharpening a never-ending supply of pencils for his lord and master. In his very limited spare time, Lambert is an avid writer, working on his romantic stories late into the night with some pencils stolen from Leonard's personal stash.

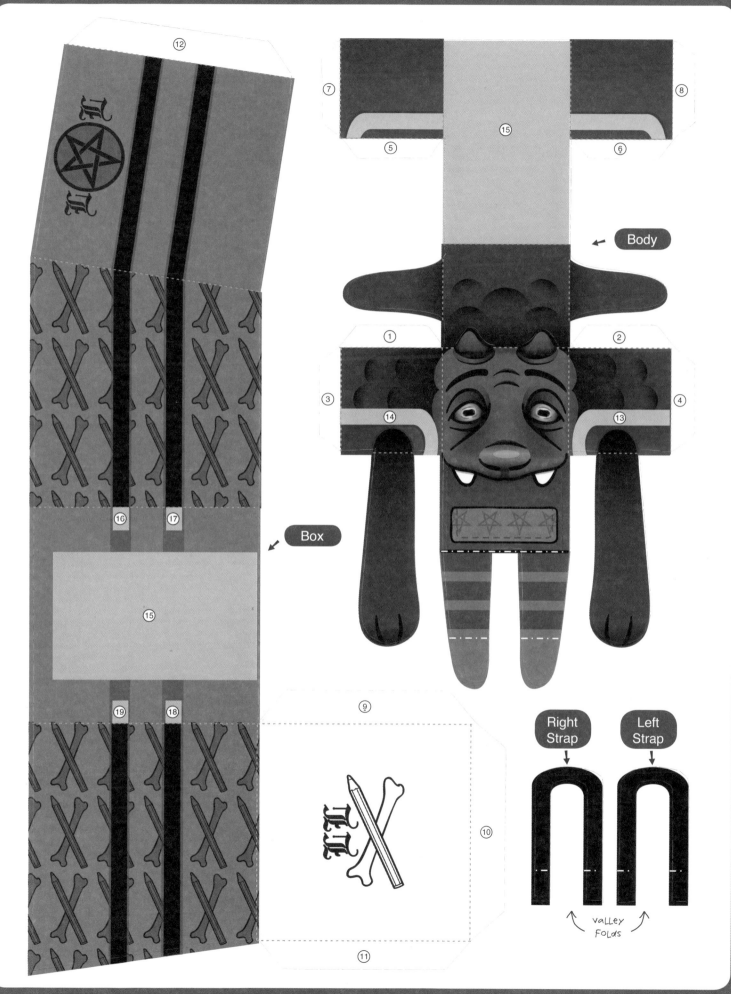

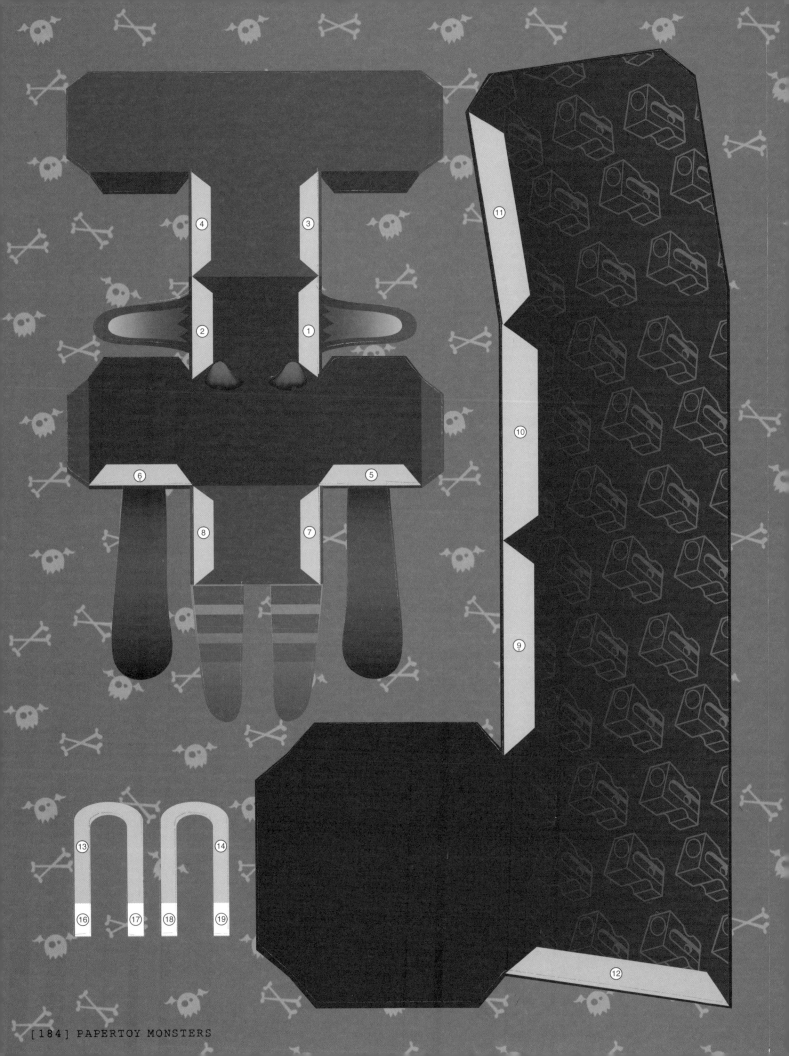

ROTTEN-BOTTOM

TYPE: *Monstrum humanus teacherus*

VARIANT NAMES: The Teacher Monster, Teacher Creature

ORIGIN: Public school in West Orange, New Jersey, U.S.A.

DESCRIPTION: 5¾ feet tall, sharp teeth, thick glasses

ABILITIES: can make time stand still; can turn any grade into a failing one

ROTTENBOTTOM

Discovered by Matt Hawkins

ASSEMBLY INSTRUCTIONS

A Detach HEAD template. Glue tabs 1–14 to gray areas 1–14.

B Detach GLASSES template. Glue GLASSES to HEAD at gray area 15.

C Detach LEFT HORN and RIGHT HORN templates. Insert tabs 16 and 17 into slots on left and right sides of HEAD.

D Detach SPIKE A and SPIKE B templates. Insert tab 18 into slot on top of HEAD. Insert tab 19 into slot on back of HEAD.

E Detach HOMEWORK template. Glue tab 20 to gray area 20 on HEAD.

F Detach UPPER BODY template. Glue tabs 21–24 to gray areas 21–24.

G Detach LOWER BODY template. Glue tabs 25–26 to gray areas 25–26.

H Glue tabs 27–30 on LOWER BODY to gray areas 27–30 on UPPER BODY. Glue

tabs 31–32 on UPPER BODY to gray areas 31–32 on LOWER BODY. Glue tabs 33–34 on LOWER BODY to gray areas 33–34 on UPPER BODY.

I Detach SPIKE C–E templates. Insert tabs 35–37 into three slots on top of UPPER BODY.

J Detach TAIL template. Insert tab 38 into slot on bottom of UPPER BODY.

K Detach RIGHT ARM template. Insert tab 39 into slot on right side of UPPER BODY.

L Detach LEFT ARM template. Insert tab 40 into slot on left side of UPPER BODY.

M Detach TIE template. Insert tab 41 into slot under chin on LOWER BODY.

N Glue tabs 42–43 on UPPER BODY to gray areas 42–43 on HEAD.

Lester Rottenbottom began his life as an ordinary human teacher who was known for his ability to make hours feel like days. Like all teachers-turned-mad-scientists, Lester was despised by his students and fellow teachers alike; he was never asked to participate in the faculty holiday party's Secret Snowflake tradition, and he was taunted in his own classroom with the usual spit wads and the classic taunts-disguised-as-coughs gag. So it was no surprise when Lester became intent on discovering a formula for turning little rats into monsters capable of taking over the world. Unfortunately for him, the experiment backfired and turned him into a paper-spewing monster. Quickly fired from his school, Lester now works as a substitute teacher, going from class to class dashing the hopes and dreams of his young students and willfully making weekends disappear by handing out large amounts of homework.

Glasses

Spike D

36

14

10

6

38

Tail

Homework

8

VALLEY FOLD

4

2

43

12

15

3

1

42

11

7

Head

16

39

Right Arm

41

Left Horn

5

Tie

17

9

40

Left Arm

Right Horn

13

23

24

Spike E

37

33

34

35

VALLEY FOLDS

Spike C

22

28

27

21

32

30

29

31

Spike B

19

25

26

18

Spike A

Lower Body

Upper Body

The Doctor

TYPE: *Monstrum humanus doctorus*

VARIANT NAME: The Mad Scientist Monster

ORIGIN: Poland

DESCRIPTION: 15 inches tall; green skin

ABILITIES: impossibly high IQ; can fit through most cat flaps

The Doctor

Discovered by Creaturekebab

ASSEMBLY INSTRUCTIONS

A Detach FRONT and RIGHT ARMS templates. Glue tabs 1–3 on RIGHT ARMS to gray areas 1–3 on FRONT.

B Detach LEFT ARMS templates. Glue tabs 4–6 to gray areas 4–6 on FRONT.

C Detach LEFT SIDE template. Curve and glue tabs 7–9 to gray areas 7–9 on FRONT.

D Detach RIGHT SIDE template. Curve and glue tabs 10–12 to gray areas 10–12 on FRONT.

E Glue RIGHT SIDE to LEFT SIDE at gray area 13.

F Detach BACK template. Glue tabs 14–19 on body piece to gray areas 14–19 on BACK.

The Doctor was at the top of his class at university, until one day he thought a glowing vial of toxic spinach was his lunch and ingested it. He instantly shrank to the size of a ferret, turned green, and grew four more arms. His fellow students and teachers found the young Doctor's predicament hysterically funny and taunted him for the remainder of his college days. Once The Doctor graduated, he swore that he'd have the last laugh and began his career as a freelance mad scientist. He is currently in the prototype phase for a project commissioned by Grumpy Gramps: to invent a mustache-producing gun so that with a single shot every living thing he passes will suddenly sprout facial whiskers. Unless you're in the market for a dashing new 'stache, it's best to avoid this particular mad scientist until this project is completed.

THE EXPERIMENT

TYPE: *Monstrum humanus mutantis*

VARIANT NAMES: The It Monster; Frankenbaby

ORIGIN: Poland

DESCRIPTION: 10 feet tall; part cat, human, moose, bird, octopus, and duck

ABILITIES: can do anything if The Doctor wills it!

THE EXPERIMENT

Discovered by Creaturekebab

ASSEMBLY INSTRUCTIONS

A Detach BODY and WING templates. Glue tab 1 on WING to gray area 1 on BODY.

B Detach LEFT PAW template. Glue tab 2 to gray area 2 on BODY.

C Detach TENTACLE template. Insert tab 3 into slot on right side of BODY and glue to gray area 3.

D Detach RIGHT PAW template. Insert tab 4 into slot on right side of BODY and glue to gray area 4.

E Glue tabs 5–8 on BODY to gray areas 5–8.

The Experiment is The Doctor's most successful nonfreelance project, created by sewing together various human and animal parts in a fit of mad creativity one stormy evening. Taking a cue from Benjamin Franklin, The Doctor brought Experiment to life by embedding a computer chip within his brain, attaching a butter knife to the top of a stack of 183 super-glued water bottles, and then leaving him out in a raging electrical storm to be struck by the first angry bolt of lightning. Thanks to the brain chip, The Doctor is constantly tinkering with Experiment, adding abilities at whim. The Experiment is extremely bright and exceptionally talented. His favorite pastimes include square dancing, fly-fishing, and belting out operatic arias.

Wing

Left Paw

Tentacle

Right Paw

Body

Lili

TYPE: *Monstrum humanus boximus*

VARIANT NAME: "Long Left" Lili

ORIGIN: The Netherlands

DESCRIPTION: 6 feet tall; humanoid; pink; jagged teeth

ABILITIES: mean double left hook, can smell a cinnamon bun from 32 miles away

Lili

Discovered by Sjors Trimbach

ASSEMBLY INSTRUCTIONS

A Detach HEAD template. Glue tabs 1–11 to gray areas 1–11.

B Detach BODY template. Glue tabs 12–18 to gray areas 12–18.

C Detach LEFT FOOT template. Glue tabs 19–22 to gray areas 19–22.

D Detach RIGHT FOOT template. Glue tabs 23–26 to gray areas 23–26.

E Insert tabs 27–28 on LEFT FOOT into slots on bottom left of BODY.

F Insert tabs 29–30 on RIGHT FOOT into slots on bottom right of BODY.

G Detach TOP RIGHT ARM template. Insert tab 31 into top slot on right side of BODY.

H Detach BOTTOM RIGHT ARM template. Insert tab 32 into bottom slot on right side of BODY.

I Detach TOP LEFT ARM template. Insert tab 33 into top slot on left side of BODY.

J Detach BOTTOM LEFT ARM template. Insert tab 34 into bottom slot on left side of BODY.

K Detach PONYTAIL template. Insert tab 35 into slot on back of HEAD.

L Glue HEAD to BODY at gray area 36.

L ili and her little sister, Paulette, were discovered deep inside the woods near Rotterdam, confused and alone, without any recollection of who or what they were. Though they are vaguely humanoid in form, no one has ever clearly ascertained whether they are monstrous humans or human-like monsters. All we do know is that these are two superstrong sisters with Muhammad Ali–like boxing skills—all wrapped up in sweet pink packages. Quite naturally, this fearsome twosome became the featured act in a traveling sideshow, in which they take on two opponents at once in a double-trouble showdown. Billed as "The Unbeatable Boxing Duo," these sisters fight in tandem, communicating with each other using a mysterious form of telepathy. "Long Left" Lili, as she came to be known, has a fierce double left hook—double because she has two left arms. And though she is blind, her heightened senses of smell and hearing allow her to smell an opponent's fear and hear his beating heart.

Paulette

TYPE: *Monstrum humanus boximus*
VARIANT NAME: *"Petite Pigtail"* Paulette
ORIGIN: The Netherlands
DESCRIPTION: 3 feet tall; pink; two long pigtails
ABILITIES: can control the movement of her pigtails; knows the first 2,001 digits of pi

Paulette

Discovered by Sjors Trimbach

ASSEMBLY INSTRUCTIONS

A Detach BODY template. Glue tabs 1–7 to gray areas 1–7.

B Detach SKIRT template. Glue tab 8 to gray area 8. Slip SKIRT over top of BODY.

C Detach RIGHT ARM template. Insert tab 9 into slot on right side of BODY.

D Detach LEFT ARM template. Insert tab 10 into slot on left side of body.

E Detach PONYTAILS templates. Insert tabs 11–12 into slots on top of BODY. Link them together if you want so they stay upright.

F Detach RIGHT FOOT template. Glue tabs 13–16 to gray areas 13–16.

G Insert tabs 17–18 on RIGHT FOOT into slots on bottom right of BODY.

H Detach LEFT FOOT template. Glue tabs 19–22 to gray areas 19–22.

I Insert tabs 23–24 on LEFT FOOT into slots on bottom left of BODY.

"**P**etite Pigtail" Paulette is one half of "The Unbeatable Boxing Duo," a mysterious and adorable pair of boxing sisters who perform in a traveling sideshow. Paulette, the younger of the two, can control her superlong, serpentine-like pigtails to knock out her opponents, both in and out of the ring. Unlike her calm and collected sister, Lili, Paulette has a bit of a short temper that has been known to flare up in a few specific situations. So if you'd like to remain conscious in her presence, it would be smart to refrain from mentioning her short and boxy shape, the current state of public education in her native Netherlands, and butterflies, which totally freak her out. When she is not boxing, Paulette can usually be found listening to heavy-metal records and thrashing her pigtails to the beat.

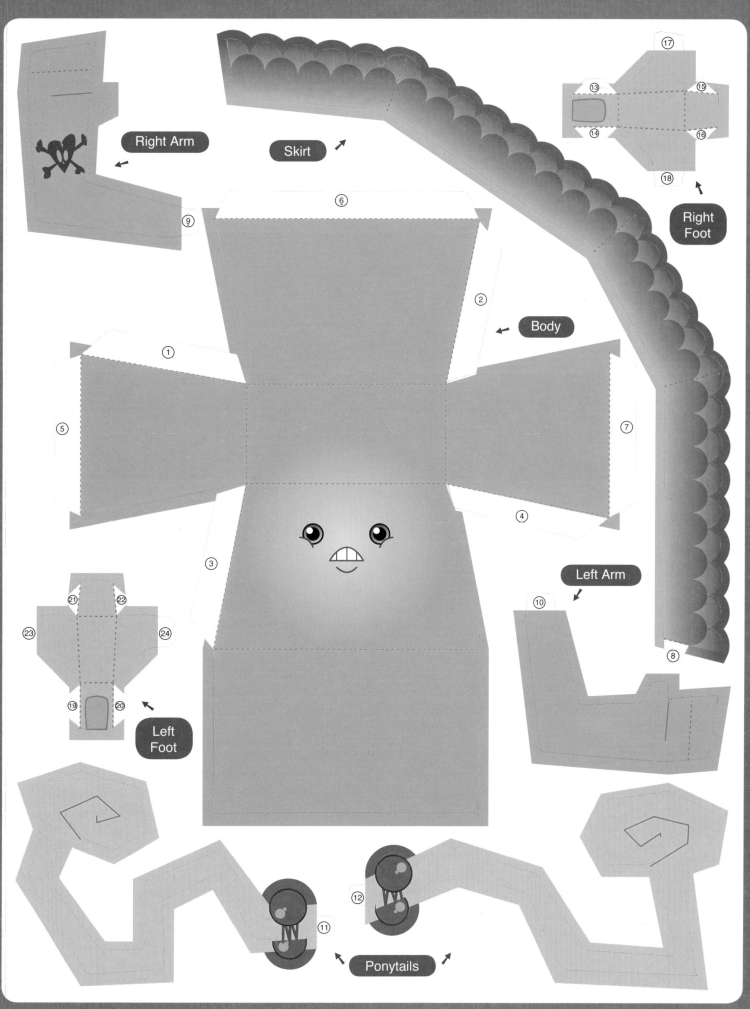

Right Arm

Skirt

Right Foot

Body

Left Arm

Left Foot

Ponytails

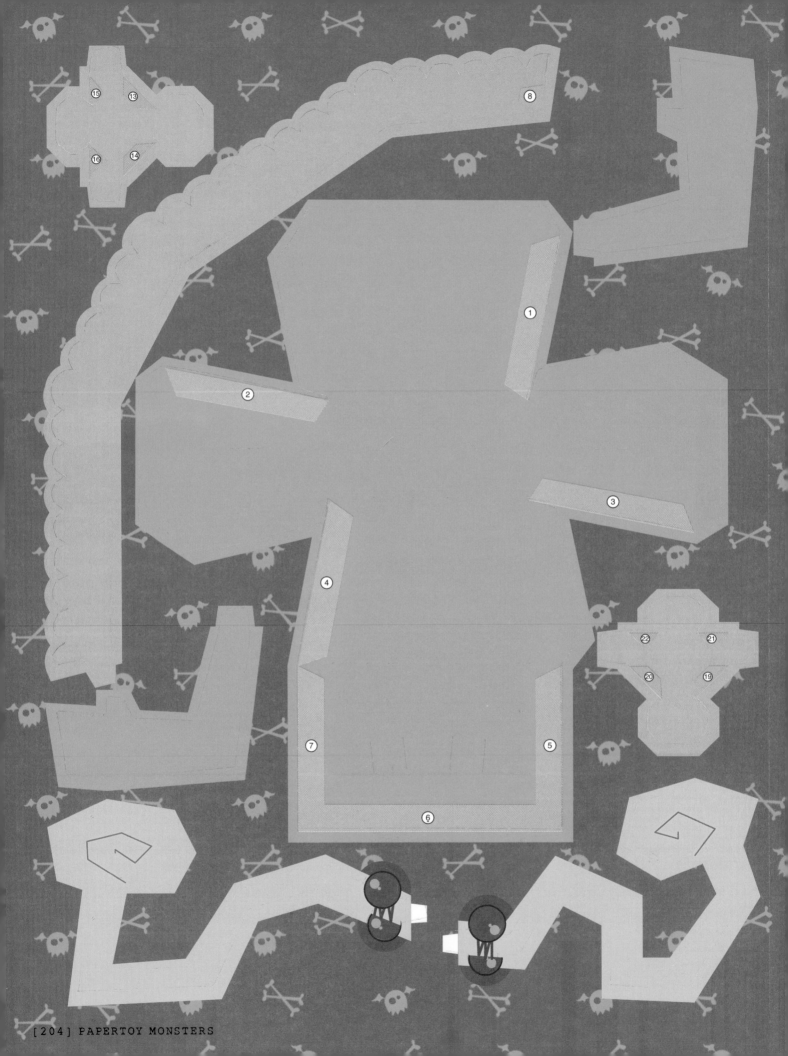

THE MONSTER KEEPERS

TYPE: *Monstrum humanus siblingus*

VARIANT NAMES: Cooper and Bella, The Dream Team

ORIGIN: Born in the U.S.A.

DESCRIPTION: 4 feet tall; adorable; nice

ABILITIES: can commune with monsters; can make 302 papertoys per hour

THE MONSTER KEEPERS

Discovered by Castleforte

ASSEMBLY INSTRUCTIONS

A Detach BODY template. Glue tabs 1–20 to gray areas 1–20.

B Detach BELLA'S COSTUME template. Insert tabs 21–22 into openings by Bella's arms between front and side of BODY.

C Detach BELLA'S MASK template. Insert tabs 23–24 into openings on sides of Bella's head between front and side of BODY.

D Detach COOPER'S COSTUME template. Insert tabs 25–26 into openings by Cooper's arms between front and side of BODY.

E Detach COOPER'S MASK template. Insert tabs 27–28 into openings on sides of Cooper's head between front and side of BODY.

F Detach BELLA'S CANDY BAG template. Glue tabs 29–30 to gray areas 29–30. Hang CANDY BAG on one arm of BELLA'S COSTUME.

Cooper and Bella, a human brother-and-sister duo, are not monsters at all. They are what we call monster keepers, children who harbor a deep respect and affection for monsters, a group largely misunderstood by society. When treated with compassion, the siblings feel, most monsters can become good citizens. In order to gain the trust and respect of the monsters they commune with, these siblings don elaborate and detailed outfits, cleverly disguised as Halloween costumes to avoid questions from prying parents. Stray baby monsters are often brought to their house for temporary foster care until they are strong enough (or old enough) to go out into the world on their own. Many of the monsters in this book have spent some time with Cooper and Bella, and even the wickedest, the filthiest, and the most horrible monsters love these gracious monster keepers.

Body

Bella's
Candy Bag

This is Bella

This is Cooper

Bella's
Mask

Cooper's
Mask

Cooper's mask
is reversible!

Bella's
Costume

Cooper's
Costume

create YOUR OWN papertoy monsters

Create-Your-Own Papertoy Monster Skins

So, you're an expert at constructing papertoy monsters designed by the spectacularly talented artists in this book, and you'd like a new challenge.

Now it's time to design your own. In the papertoy community, artists often create blank templates and invite fans to bring the toy to life with their own designs. This process is called "skinning," and each new design is a new "skin."

On the following pages, you'll find blank templates of monsters you've encountered before—but this time, *you* get to decide what they look like.

- Draw, color, paint, or create a collage.

- Make it realistic, abstract, or somewhere in between.

- Give your monster a mini-biography: Think up a backstory, special abilities, and alternate names.

IT'S ALL UP TO YOU.

Just follow the simple directions below and use your imagination to create your perfect papertoy.

INSTRUCTIONS

DRAW your design directly onto the template.

REFER to the pages listed at the top of each template for assembly instructions.

HINT: You may want to scan or photocopy the template first so that you can experiment until you've perfected your creation.

This is a blank template of Icy Huggy. Refer to the assembly instructions on page 4.

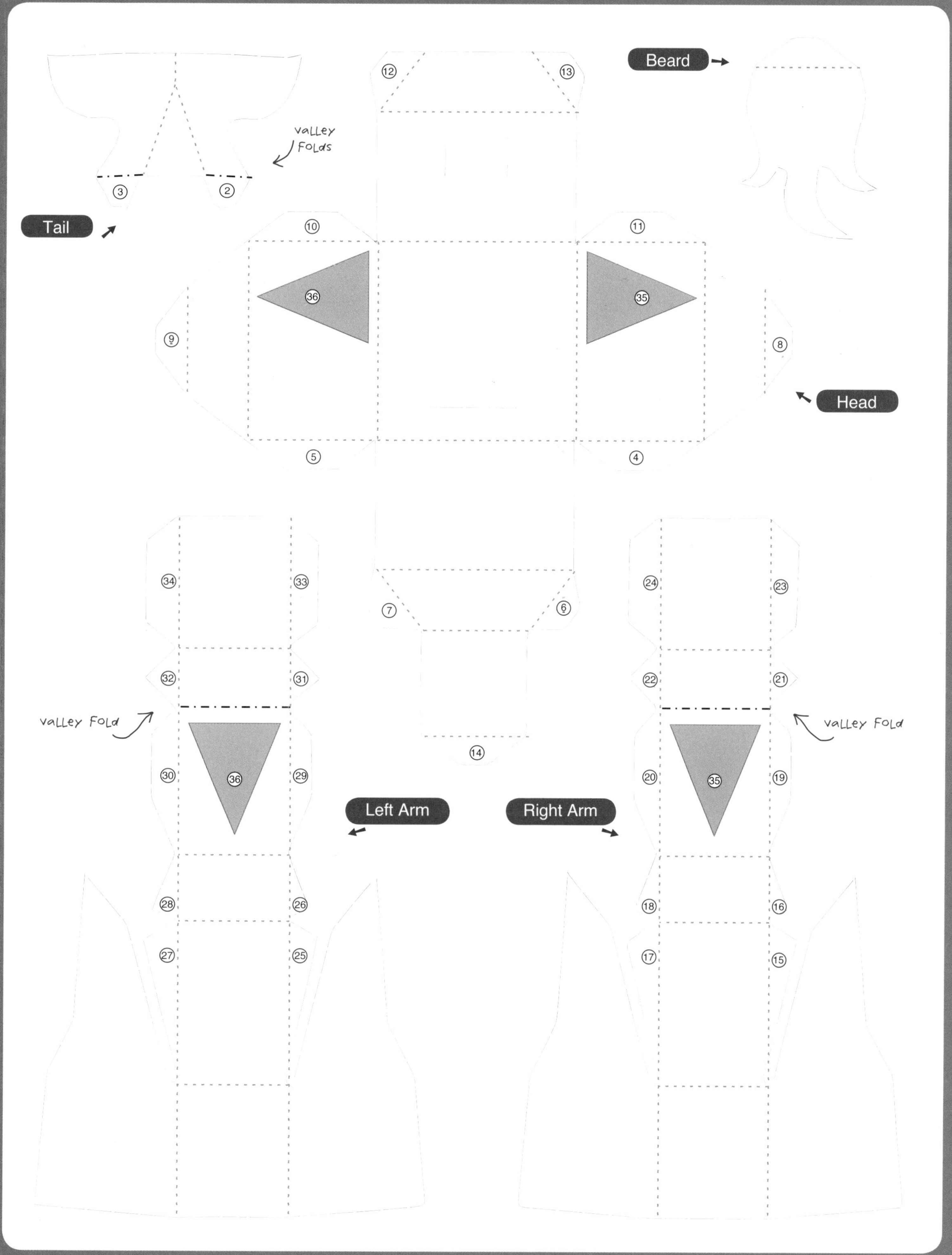

Beard
Tail
valley Folds
Head
valley Fold
valley Fold
Left Arm
Right Arm

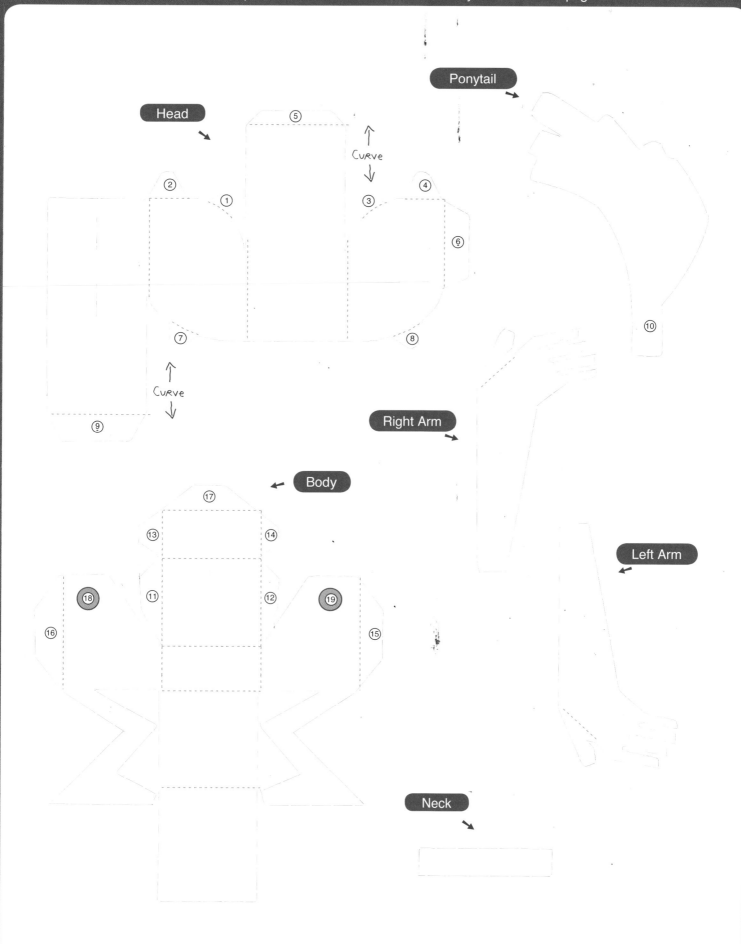

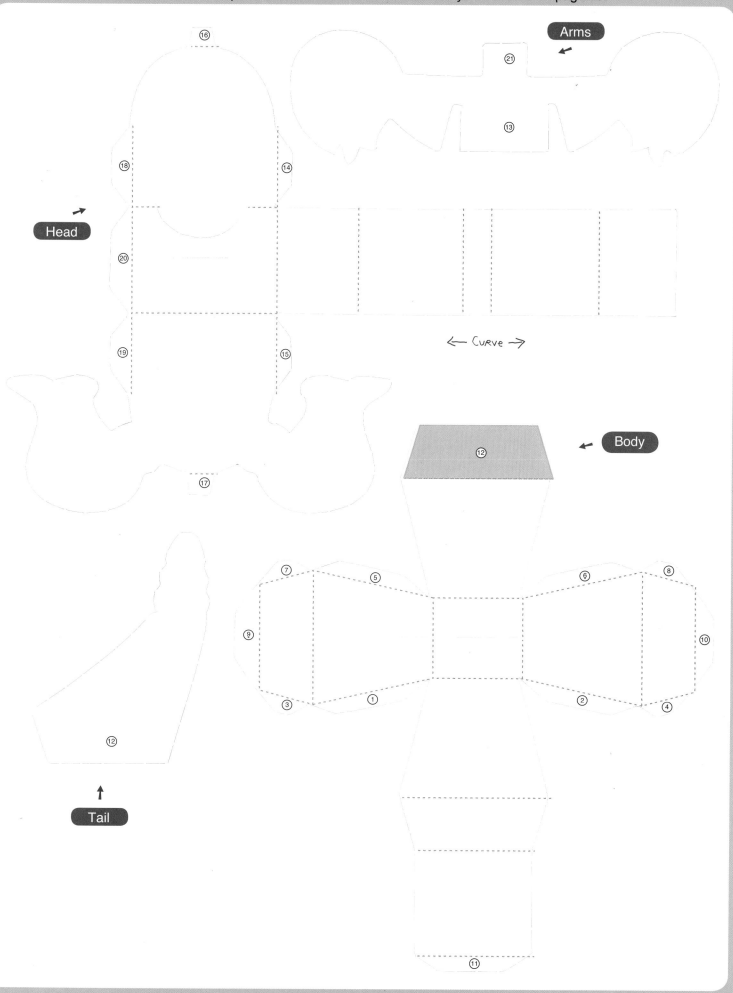

Arms

Head

← Curve →

Body

Tail

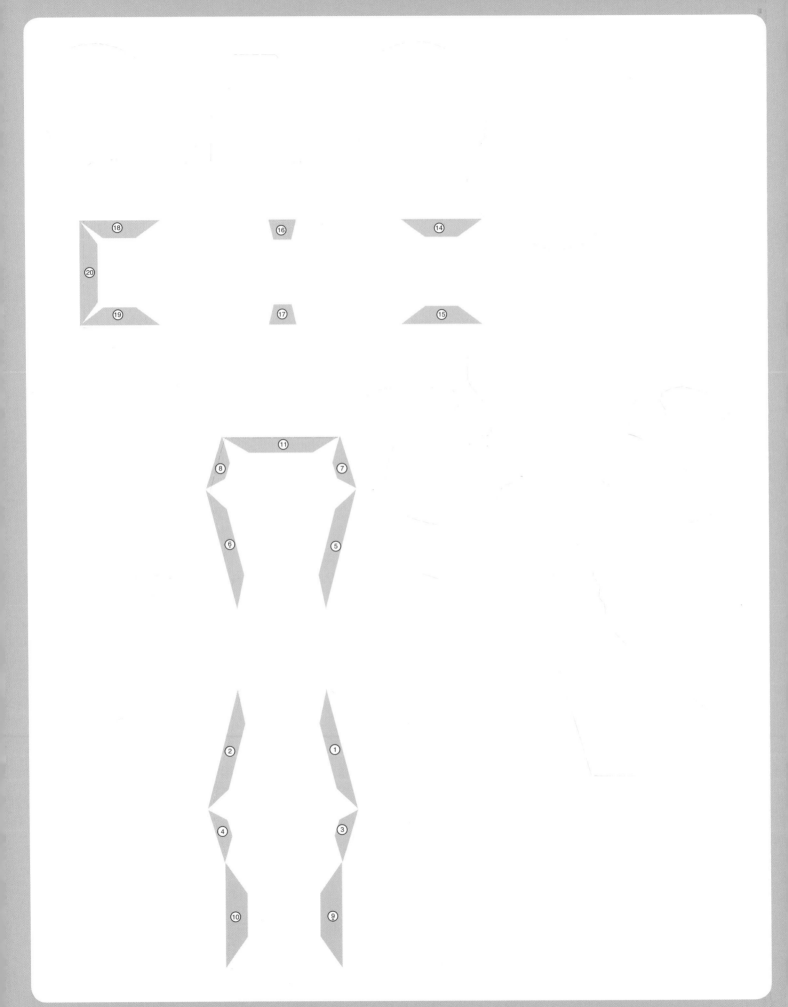

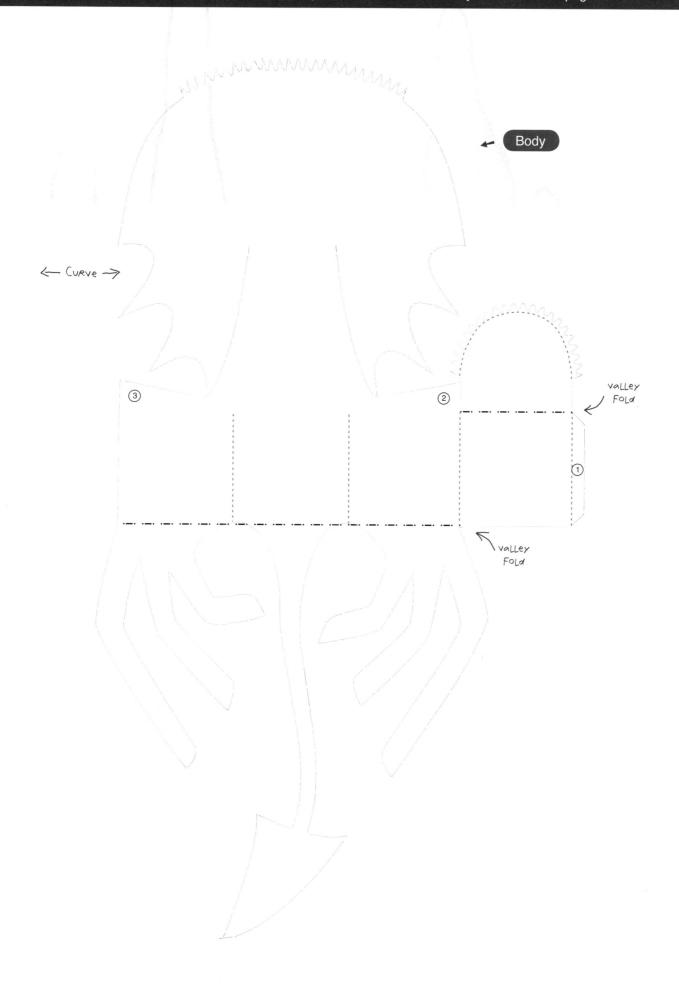

Body

← Curve →

③

②

①

valley fold

valley fold

This is a blank template of Mega Larb. Refer to the assembly instructions on page 90.

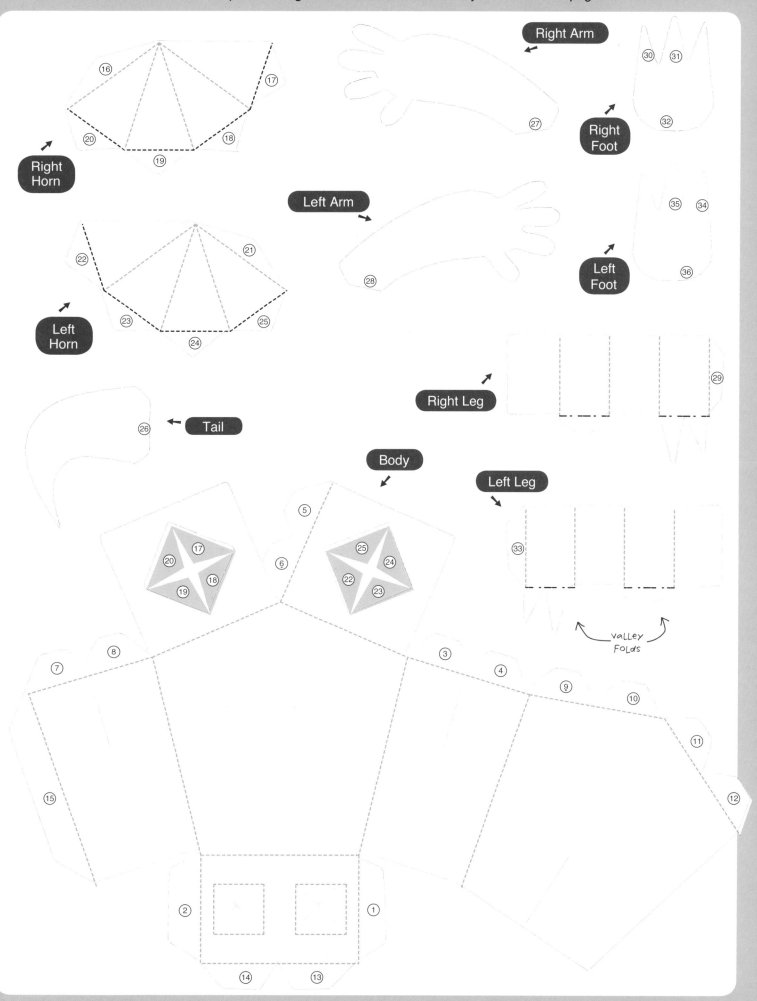

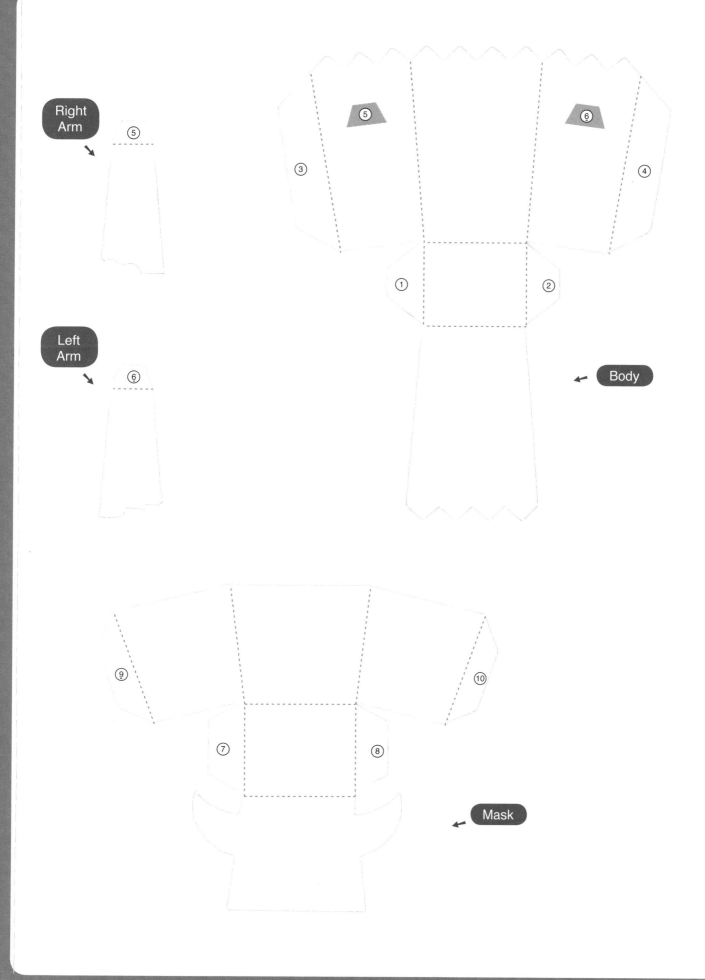

Right Arm

⑤

Left Arm

⑥

③ ⑤ ⑥ ④

① ②

Body

⑨ ⑩

⑦ ⑧

Mask

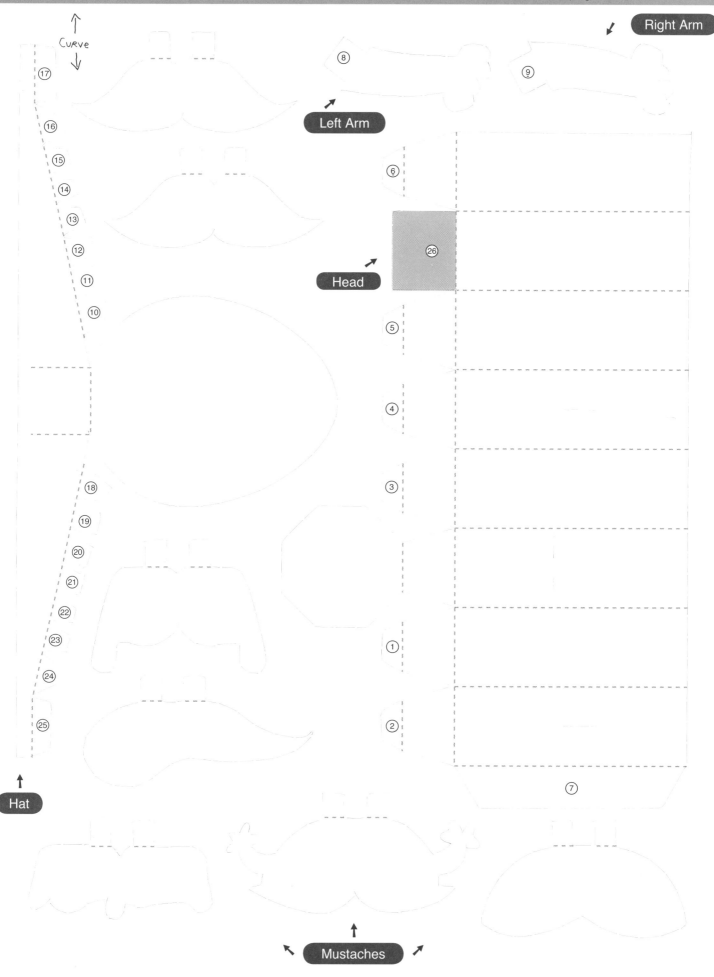

Right Arm

Curve

⑰

⑯

⑮

⑭

⑬

⑫

⑪

⑩

⑱

⑲

⑳

㉑

㉒

㉓

㉔

㉕

Hat

⑧

Left Arm

⑨

⑥

㉖

⑤

④

③

①

②

⑦

Head

Mustaches

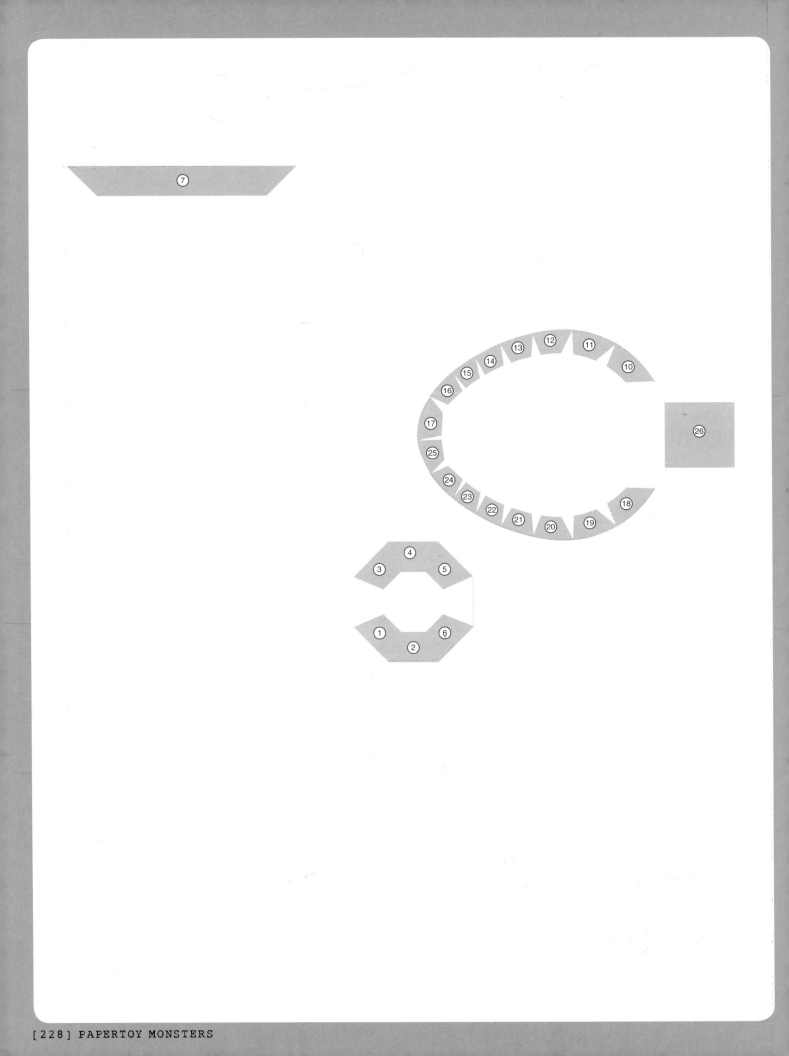

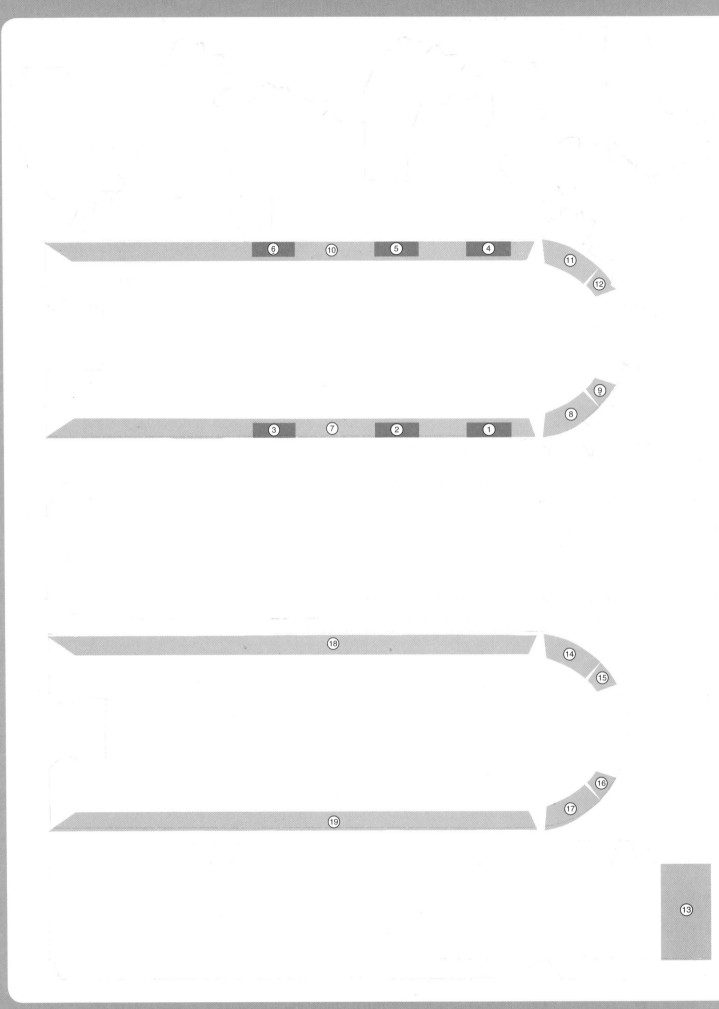